I0815417

BRINGING HEAVEN HERE

BRINGING HEAVEN HERE

How THE LORD'S PRAYER *Can* CHANGE YOUR LIFE *and* OUR WORLD

BRAD GRAY

and BRAD NELSON

W Publishing Group

An Imprint of Thomas Nelson

Bringing Heaven Here

Published by W Publishing, an imprint of Thomas Nelson, 501 Nelson Place, Nashville, TN 37214, USA.

The author is represented by Alive Literary Agency, www.aliveliterary.com.

Thomas Nelson titles may be purchased in bulk for educational, business, fundraising, or sales promotional use. For information, please email SpecialMarkets@ThomasNelson.com.

ISBN 978-1-4002-5276-3 (audiobook)
ISBN 978-1-4002-5275-6 (ePub)
ISBN 978-1-4002-5268-8 (hardcover)

HarperCollins Publishers, Macken House, 39/40 Mayor Street Upper, Dublin 1, D01 C9W8, Ireland (https://www.harpercollins.com)

Library of Congress Control Number: 2025942534

Art Direction and Cover Design: Meg Schmidt
Interior Design: Kristy Edwards

Printed in the United States of America

25 26 27 28 29 LBC 5 4 3 2 1

To Denyon, Aryah, Calyx, and Xyler, may this prayer guide you daily for the rest of your lives. I love you and I'm proud of you!

—Brad Gray

To Mom and Dad, thank you for living the words of this prayer so well.

—Brad Nelson

THE LORD'S PRAYER
(AUTHORS' VERSION)

Our Father in the heavens,
holy be your name.
Your kingdom come,
your will be done,
on earth as it is in heaven.
Give us this day our daily bread.
And forgive us our debts,
as we also have forgiven our debtors.
And lead us not into temptation,
but deliver us from evil.
For yours is the kingdom and the power
and the glory forever. Amen.

CONTENTS

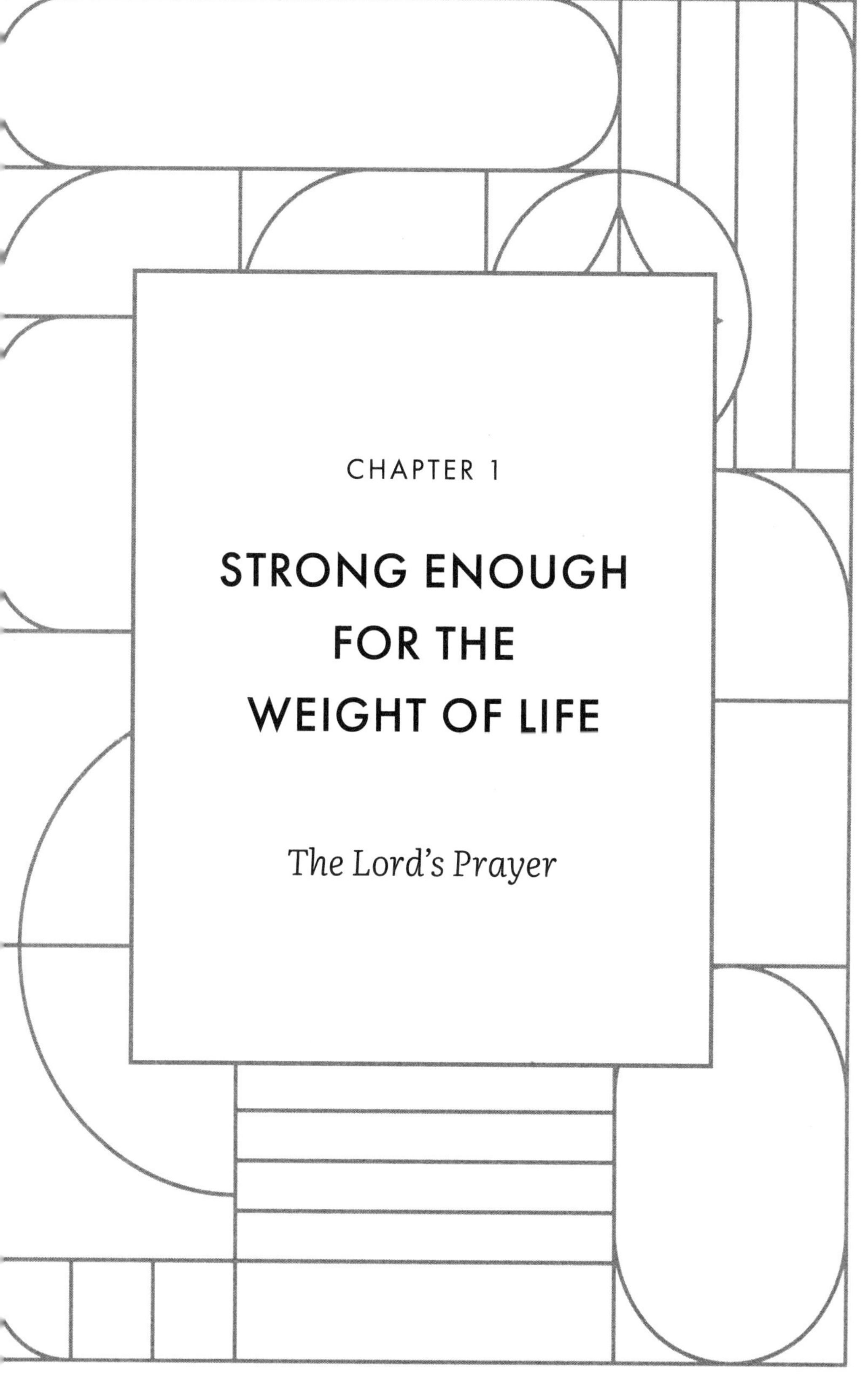

CHAPTER 1

STRONG ENOUGH FOR THE WEIGHT OF LIFE

The Lord's Prayer

BRAD GRAY

If the world feels louder, faster, angrier, lonelier, and more divided than you remember, it's not just you. Institutions are fraying. Attention spans are shrinking. Change is accelerating faster than we know how to respond. The sheer volume of information we absorb each day exceeds our ability to process or make meaning of it—leaving us anxious, distracted, and depleted.

You'd think all that information and connection would lead to deeper understanding and more meaningful relationships. Instead, we curate which voices we want to hear and filter out those we don't, creating echo chambers that fuel an increasingly polarized and tribal world.

And just beneath the surface, there's a collective unease we can't quite shake. We've lived through a global pandemic that forced millions of people to rearrange how they live, work, and connect almost overnight. We've endured waves of economic instability, the heartbreak of school shootings, and a widespread decline in mental health that touches nearly every family. These disruptions haven't just made life harder—they've made it harder to trust, to rest, to feel safe. Perhaps not surprisingly, in May 2023, then US Surgeon General Vivek Murthy declared loneliness and isolation a public health crisis.[1]

It's no wonder so many of us feel untethered. The center—the place of meaning, belonging, truth—feels blurred, contested, weaponized, or forgotten. We sense it in our relationships, our institutions, even in our own hearts. Something is falling apart.

More than a century ago, in the aftermath of World War I, poet William Butler Yeats wrote words that land with startling relevance today: "Things fall apart; the centre cannot hold; mere anarchy is loosed upon the world."[2]

We're not simply exhausted. We're *unmoored.*

And the world isn't the only thing that's changing. So is our faith—at least the way we practice it. You've seen the stats. People are walking away from the church in droves. Not out of rebellion, but out of disillusionment, fatigue, and a deep hunger for something *more.* But beneath all the cynicism, there's still a longing: a hunger for something ancient and rooted. Something true.

For many, the forms of faith we inherited can't sustain the weight of the life we're facing. So, quietly, desperately, we search for a way to begin again.

In a world this disoriented, we're not just looking for relief—we're looking for a way to live. A rhythm. A framework. A path that's ancient enough to trust and practical enough to walk.

That's exactly what Jesus offered when he gave his disciples—and us—the Lord's Prayer. It's the most well-known prayer in human history.[3]

You'll hear it recited in churches, hospitals, military barracks, and locker rooms. Most people—whether they're religious or not—are familiar with it. But for Jesus' first followers, it was significantly more than just a prayer; it was a blueprint for daily life, shaping their identity and guiding how they lived.

As theologians William Willimon and Stanley Hauerwas wrote, "The church traditionally instructed new Christians by teaching them this prayer. . . . So if you are asked, 'Who is a Christian?' the best answer you can give is, 'Someone who has learned to pray the Lord's Prayer.'"[4] This wasn't about performing a memorization exercise. It was about reordering their lives around the heartbeat of heaven.

Likewise, Jesus doesn't mean for us simply to recite the prayer; he means for us to live it.

In Jesus' day, when a rabbi (or sage) gave their disciples a specific prayer, it was seen as an invitation to take part in God's work. Prayer wasn't passive; it was collaborative. The disciples understood they had a role to play in bringing that prayer to fruition. The same is true with the Lord's Prayer. Every line was a call to align their lives with what God was doing in the world.

And it wasn't just something Jesus taught his disciples to pray; it was the very prayer he was living out in his own life.

When you grasp its depth and breadth, you'll see why the Lord's Prayer is the single most important passage in the Bible for understanding who God is, why Jesus came, and what we're doing here on earth. It's a condensed summary of Jesus' entire life and ministry. If you want to understand Jesus—if you want to share in the kind and quality of life he lived—understand his prayer.

What's more, the Lord's Prayer encapsulates the story of the Bible. When you understand this prayer, not only does it unleash the power of Scripture, but it *unlocks you*—revealing your purpose on earth and your role in God's mission. I believe that pondering and praying this prayer is the most important practice a follower of Jesus can do every day!

But somehow, I missed this.

I've been following Jesus for nearly forty years. My parents did an amazing job guiding me into an awareness of him as a child, and I've spent most of my adult life helping others do the same. I served as a pastor for a decade. I've led study trips to the Middle East for more than fifteen years, taught thousands of people how to read the Bible in context, and created a nonprofit organization designed to help Scripture come alive for people.

I could always recite the Lord's Prayer—with its thees, thys, and arts—but I didn't always pray it, at least not regularly or meaningfully. Yet, when Jesus told his disciples, "This, then, is how you should pray," I think he meant it (Matthew 6:9).

So did the early church. According to the *Didache*, a discipleship manual dating to the late first century or early second century AD, followers of Jesus were instructed to pray the Lord's Prayer three times a day![5]

They anchored their days around this prayer, believing it was the single most important practice for forming them into the people of God.

It's meant to form us as well.

Seven years ago, something shifted in my life, and I began to realize why the Lord's Prayer is so central. At first, it was an insight here, a connection there; then it became like an avalanche. I started seeing God differently. I began to experience his presence in ways I hadn't noticed before.

Slowly, the prayer started shaping me, rewiring how I thought, how I interacted with others, and what I gave my attention to.

And once I saw it, I couldn't unsee it.

Again, this was a prayer Jesus not only taught but also lived—and, if we let it, it will reshape how we live too.

Okay, you might be thinking, *if the Lord's Prayer is so powerful, why don't we experience it that way?*

WHY WE MISS IT

I'm guessing you can recite the words too. Maybe you learned them as a kid like I did. That's actually one of the problems: *familiarity.*

When something becomes too familiar, we can assume we have it mastered and begin overlooking it altogether. Philosopher Dallas Willard once observed that, in essence, when people think they already understand Jesus, their "presumed familiarity has led to unfamiliarity, and unfamiliarity has led to contempt."[6]

That's the irony: The very prayer Jesus gave to anchor our lives has become background noise. We mumble it at church services, weddings, and funerals—moments that should feel charged with the holy, but instead, they feel routine, safe, and sanitized. When that happens, we don't just lose the prayer's meaning; we lose its power.

A few years ago, I was digging through some boxes in the attic and found my old iPod. Remember those? Miraculously, it still worked. I spent the whole weekend listening to playlists I hadn't touched in years. I knew every word, and yet, the songs *felt* new. Of course, the lyrics hadn't changed. But I had.

That's how it works with things we think we already know. An old line, a familiar phrase, a longtime friend—suddenly we hear them with fresh ears or see them with fresh eyes, and it's like discovering them all over again.

The Lord's Prayer was meant to be not a script but a summons to bold, subversive acts of faith. So how do we recover the force of something we think we already know?

We start with context.

By context, I mean the world behind the text itself—the history, culture, geography, language, literary design, and even the visual backdrops that shaped how the original hearers would've understood the words.

The biblical writers didn't spell everything out because they didn't have to. Their audiences already knew the references, places, and backstories Jesus' words would have evoked. But we're not ancient readers; we're modern ones, thousands of years and miles removed. So, as I like to say, "Every time we open the Bible, we're engaging in a cross-cultural experience."[7] And if we forget that, we risk bringing our assumptions, language, and worldview to a text that wasn't written in our time or culture.

Without context, we're prone to misunderstanding—or worse, misusing—the text altogether. As one rabbi explained to Eugene Peterson, "If you don't understand it rightly, you'll obey it wrongly—and your obedience will be disobedience."[8]

That's not just poetic. It's sobering. Getting the Bible wrong can mean getting life wrong.

We all know what it feels like to have our words taken out of context, and this happens with the Bible all the time. Too often, our first question when reading is: "What does this mean for me, right now?" It's a fair question. It's just not the first one we should be asking.

The better first question is: What did this mean to them, then?

If we can begin there, something shifts. The Bible becomes less confusing and more compelling. Familiar passages get new depth. Unfamiliar ones open up with surprising relevance. This is why I've given my life to helping people encounter the Bible in its original context.

When we uncover the world behind the prayer, we'll recover the power within it.

The familiar, often-glossed-over prayer will begin to pulsate with new life.

ABOUT THE TWO BRADS

This book is coauthored by two best friends who happen to share the same first name. I go by Brad, and he goes by Nelson. We met as freshmen at Cornerstone University. Almost immediately, we realized we were chasing the same kind of life. That shared pursuit sparked a friendship that has shaped both of us ever since.

We both served as captains on our collegiate sports teams—Nelson, soccer, and me, basketball. We led a Bible study on campus, attended the same seminary, and eventually both became pastors. Over the years, we've walked with each other through weddings, funerals, miscarriages and other losses, and all the highs and lows in between. I often joke that Nelson is the other half of my brain. If I'm ever stuck on a teaching, he's my first call.

A few years ago, he joined me at Walking The Text, the nonprofit organization I started in 2018. We both lead study trips to the Bible lands, write and present *The Teaching Series*,[9] and create projects like *The Lord's Prayer* film and *The Sacred Thread* series—and now, this book.

To keep things clear, we've divided each phrase of the Lord's Prayer into two chapters—one from each of us. At the beginning of every chapter, we'll let you know who's writing and whose stories you're stepping into.[10]

Different voices. Same name. Same heartbeat.

WHY WE WROTE THIS BOOK

When we created *The Lord's Prayer* film and season one of *The Sacred Thread*, we explored the rich contextual backdrop of the prayer. But there's only so much you can fit into a film and television series. We didn't have space to unpack the countless moments, insights, and implications for everyday life in the prayer—the ones that touch how you handle conflict, respond to pain, make decisions, take responsibility, or pray when you're not even sure God's listening.

That's what this book is for.

It offers not just clarity but courage. Not just comfort but calling. In a noisy, disorienting world, it will show you how the Lord's Prayer can recenter your life around what matters most.

If you've felt like your faith can't bear the weight of your real life, if you've ever wanted to start over with God but didn't know how, if you're hungry for something deeper than performance, more grounded than hype, and more human than religious clichés, this book was written for you.

Along the way, we hope you'll laugh out loud. Because God didn't design life to be heavy all the time.

We hope you'll tear up. Because this prayer speaks to real pain, not polite problems.

We hope you'll say, "Wait, what?! I never knew that!" Because context changes everything.

And most of all, we hope you'll find yourself utterly transfixed by Jesus—and awakened to a way of life that's both ancient and astonishingly new.

At the heart of this prayer is the realization that salvation isn't just about going to heaven when we die; it's about partnering with God to bring heaven here. Salvation isn't the finish line—it's the starting line for a life of courageous discipleship.

In the pages ahead, we'll take each phrase of the Lord's Prayer and explore what it meant in its original context and what it means for your life right now. We believe that with modern stories, ancient perspectives, and fresh insights, these chapters will awaken your heart, renew your trust, and invite you to walk more closely with Jesus. He has used this prayer to change lives for two thousand years, helping people reimagine broken stories and reigniting their weary hearts. We expect he will use it to do the same for you.

Our hope is that you'll never go another day of your life without saying this prayer.

So let's begin where Jesus did: with *our Father.*

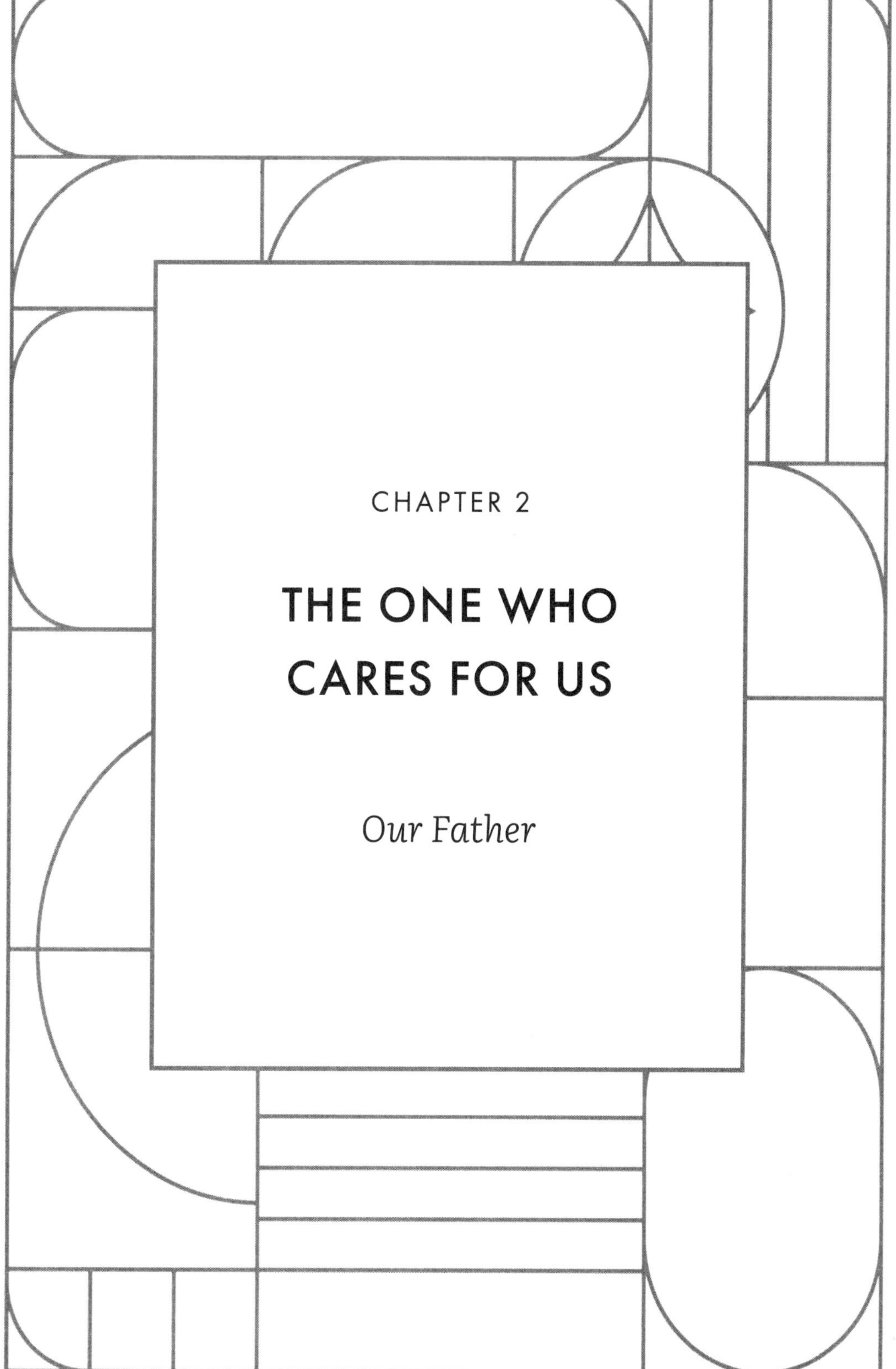

CHAPTER 2

THE ONE WHO CARES FOR US

Our Father

BRAD GRAY

My wife, Shallon, and I have four children, and I love being their dad. It's the greatest privilege and responsibility of my life. I do my best to love them well—but more often than I'd like to admit, I completely misread what they need.

One of the first challenges I faced as a parent was learning to decode their cries. At first they all sounded like, *The world is ending!* But over time, I started to notice subtle differences.

There was the *I'm hungry* cry.

The *I'm overtired and need to sleep* cry.

The *I really need a diaper change* cry.

And—worst of all—the *I'm in pain* cry.

Each had its own tone and urgency, and I had to learn them all, since crying is the only way infants can say, *See me. Help me. Hold me.*

Author and psychiatrist Curt Thompson wrote, "We're all born into the world looking for someone who is looking for us, and we remain in this mode for the rest of our lives."[1] There's never a time when we stop searching for a wise and loving presence, someone who can see into our pain and confusion, even when we don't fully understand it ourselves or know exactly what we need. When a parent responds to a child's needs, they lay a foundation for a life of meaningful connection—the same kind of connection Jesus invites us into when we pray.

This is why Jesus didn't begin the Lord's Prayer with lofty divine titles or elaborate requests, but with relationship. We can see it in two simple words: *Our Father.*

Prayer is the vulnerable act of turning toward the one who knows us better than we know ourselves and asking, "Will you see me?"

But we're no fools. We don't open our hearts to just anybody. We reveal them only to those who've earned the right, and if we're going to pray, we need to know who we're praying to.

A. W. Tozer once famously wrote, "What comes into our minds when we think about God is the most important thing about us."[2] Why? Because what we think God is like not only shapes who we become; it shapes whether we approach him at all.

So when Jesus begins this prayer, he invites us to see God as "our Father." For those of us blessed with a healthy father-child relationship, addressing God this way isn't an issue.

I'm one of those fortunate people who has an amazing relationship with my dad. Despite our height difference—he's six foot four and I'm five foot nine (yes, I got robbed!)—we look eerily alike. We have the same build, bald head, and deep-set eyes. For a time, I acquired the nickname "Mini-Me" when the Austin Powers films were making their rounds in the late 1990s. Like I said, Dad and I look eerily alike. The congruence of our physical features extends to our relationship as well. We've always been tight, and he's one of my closest friends. He's always been there for me, caring, challenging, and encouraging me in everything I do. My story makes it easy for me to see God as a "Father."

But for many people, these two words—*Our Father*—bring pain instead of comfort. Over the years, I've heard stories like these again and again:

"My dad walked out on us when I was a kid, and we haven't heard from him since."

"I could never live up to my dad's expectations."

"My dad and I don't have a great relationship. He's always been emotionally distant."

"My dad was violent. I felt unsafe around the one person who was supposed to protect me."

If anything like this is part of your story, it's completely understandable that calling God "Father" might feel more like a barrier than a blessing. If that's you, my heart aches with yours. Your pain matters. The hardship you've endured and the ways you've been wounded aren't something to gloss over.

But they don't have to be the lens through which you see God.

The good news is, your experience with your dad (or lack of one) was never meant to define who God is. God is not a reflection of your earthly father. He's the perfection of everything a father was meant to be.

That's why the starting point isn't your earthly father, but the God revealed in Scripture as "Father." Seeing God for who he truly is can reframe everything. To begin doing that, we need to go back to the very first place in the Bible where God identifies himself as a Father.

It's not a sweet, sentimental moment, but a moment of deep suffering.

THE FATHER WHO HEARS AND RESCUES

The Bible isn't just a collection of ancient, inspired texts. It's a unified story, stitched together by divine threads that all come together in Jesus. So when a word or theme appears for the first time in the story, it's never accidental. It's a signal. It sets the stage for everything that follows, which is why it's so important to pay attention to where it first appears in Scripture.[3] This is called the "principle of first use,"[4] and it isn't a fancy or sophisticated modern method for interpreting the Bible. It's how Jesus' audience read the Scriptures.

When Jesus said the words "Our Father," his audience wouldn't have thought of their own fathers. Their memories would've raced back to the exodus story when their ancestors were slaves in Egypt, owned by Pharaoh and forced to make bricks in the blazing sun. Brickmaking was backbreaking work: dredging mud from the Nile; mixing it with water, manure, and straw; slapping it into wooden frames; and then letting the bricks bake for two weeks.[5] In Pharaoh's eyes, they were only as valuable as what they could produce. If they worked, they had purpose; if not, they were disposable.

It was horrific. It was evil. And the Bible tells us the people were in anguish.

"The Israelites groaned in their slavery and *cried out*, and their cry for help because of their slavery went up to God. God *heard* their groaning and he *remembered* his covenant with Abraham, with Isaac and with Jacob. So God looked on the Israelites and was *concerned* about them" (Exodus 2:23–25, emphasis added).

They cried out.

God heard.

God remembered.[6]

God was concerned.

The Israelites' groaning elicited a divine response. When God appeared to Moses at the burning bush, he confirmed this: "I have indeed seen . . . I have heard . . . I am concerned . . . so I have come down to rescue" (Exodus 3:7–8).

In his first encounter with the living God of the universe, Moses learned that God not only cares about people in need but is willing to do something about it. What's more, Moses discovered that he had a role to play in God's rescue plan—one that required him to return to Egypt, march into Pharaoh's palace, and demand that he let God's people go.

What made God's call all the more staggering was that the last time Moses had seen Egypt, he'd been a fugitive.

If you're familiar with the exodus story, none of this is surprising. But there's a small, often-overlooked detail embedded in the message God gave Moses to deliver to Pharaoh, and it's the very detail Jesus was drawing on in the Lord's Prayer: "Say to Pharaoh, 'This is what the LORD says: Israel is my firstborn son, and I told you, "Let my son go, so he may worship me"'" (Exodus 4:22–23).

Did you catch that?

"Israel is my firstborn son."

With that statement, God revealed something about himself: *He is a Father*. Not a distant or detached one, but one who hears the cries of his children and turns up in the middle of their pain, ready to rescue. The first time God named himself as a Father, it wasn't in a moment of comfort or triumph, but in the anguish of slavery.

That's what Jesus was drawing on when he taught us to pray, "Our Father."

At its core, God's fatherhood is about more than compassion; it's about deliverance. He hears. He sees. He comes down.

God gave Moses a glimpse of this at the burning bush, and then he did something even more intimate: For the first time in all of Scripture, God revealed his personal name.

THE FATHER WHO MAKES HIMSELF KNOWN

When you walk into a room full of people you don't know, you typically start by saying your name and asking for theirs. It's a common experience that doesn't feel particularly meaningful, but this wouldn't have been the case in the ancient world.

Back then, a name was much more than a label. It revealed your identity and your destiny, the essence of who you were and who you were becoming. To know someone's name was to know something deep about who they truly were. That's why it mattered so much when God revealed his name to Moses.

According to Dr. Carmen Joy Imes, "The gods of the ancient world were mysterious and cryptic, often known by a pseudonym that kept others at arm's length."[7] But not the God of the Bible. He didn't pull back from his people; he stepped forward. He made himself known. And he still does today.

At the burning bush, God revealed his personal name to Moses when he said, "I AM WHO I AM. This is what you are to say to the Israelites: 'I AM has sent me to you'" (Exodus 3:14).[8]

Then he added, "Say to the Israelites, 'The LORD, the God of your fathers—the God of Abraham, the God of Isaac and the God of Jacob—has sent me to you.' This is my name forever, the name you shall call me from generation to generation" (Exodus 3:15).

The proper name given here is *Yahweh,*[9] rendered as "LORD" in this passage, but prefaced with the much longer phrase, "I AM WHO I AM." This also can be translated as "I WILL BE WHAT I WILL BE" or "WHAT WILL BE WILL BE."[10]

In other words, "You'll know what I'm like by what I'm about to do."

It's a powerful way to understand who God is, because what he does next is rescue his people from slavery in Egypt! It's as if God was saying, "I want people to know for generations to come that the essence of who I am is someone who rescues and redeems people in their time of need. I am a God who hears. A God who sees. A God who saves."

After that, God spoke of Israel as his son, placing himself in the position of Father, making the connection profoundly clear: God is the kind of Father who listens to his children, knows what they need, and is willing to act.

So to the Israelites, "Father" signified care and concern.

Rescue and redemption.

Family and belonging.

And it's the foundation for understanding the beginning of the Lord's Prayer. Jesus knew his audience would immediately connect the dots, drawing on the rich history of God as their Father.

What about you? When you hear the word *Father,* do you imagine someone distant? Angry? Disinterested? Or do you picture someone who knows you—really knows you—and wants to draw near?

How you see God shapes how you speak to him. Envisioning God as a distant or angry deity can lead you to pray with fear, hoping to get it right. But seeing him as a loving Father can allow you to speak with trust. Beginning your prayers with "Our Father" can help reshape your view of God, especially as you remember that God promised to rescue his people—and he did. It can ground you in who your Father truly is because it draws from what he has already done.

Consider how God not only delivered his people from Egypt but also stayed close and cared for them throughout the ages, even in difficult times.

In the desert, he promised Moses that one day he would set his people free again, saying, "I will raise up for them a prophet like you [Moses] from among their fellow Israelites, and I will put my words in his mouth. He will tell them everything I command him. I myself will call to account anyone who does not listen to my words that the prophet speaks in my name" (Deuteronomy 18:18–19).

That vision of a coming prophet sustained Israel's hope. Generations passed, and the promise of a coming prophet echoed throughout the centuries. Israel endured exile, conquest, and hundreds of years of domination by foreign empires. And still, they waited with hope.

By the first century, their longing had only intensified. Living under the boot of the Roman Empire, many were left wondering, *When will God set us free like he did in the exodus?*

That's when crowds of the sick, hurting, and dispossessed began flocking to a Jewish rabbi and finding life. His signs, wonders, and teachings all seemed to be following a familiar script, like his life was telling a story the Jews already knew.

People began to wonder, *Is he a prophet? Could he be* the *Prophet who will lead us out of exile and back into freedom?*

It was in this cultural moment that Jesus, surrounded by crowds, turned to his disciples and uttered the words, "This, then, is how you should pray: 'Our Father . . .'" (Matthew 6:9).

With those two words, Jesus ignited their Scripture-soaked memories. When they heard "Our Father," they heard "freedom."

THE FATHER WHO FOLLOWS THROUGH

The story Jesus was telling with his life, the one that set the disciples' hearts ablaze, was an exodus story. They came to realize that he was indeed the one they'd been waiting for—the Prophet, the second Moses, the Messiah, the coming King of Israel. Jesus was leading a rescue mission, and Matthew framed his story to echo the exodus at every turn.

When King Herod began his murderous hunt for the infant Jesus, God prompted Joseph to flee Bethlehem with his family and find safety in Egypt. They remained in Egypt until Herod died. You may know this story well—but do you know the remarkable statement Matthew made about it?

"And so was fulfilled what the Lord had said through the prophet: 'Out of Egypt I called my son'" (Matthew 2:15).

"Out of Egypt I called my son" is a direct quote from Hosea 11:1, recorded more than seven hundred years before Jesus' birth. Intriguingly, the original context of this passage has nothing to do with Jesus—so on the surface, it seems like a stretch. Why would Matthew quote a verse about Israel and apply it to Jesus? Was it a misstep? Did Matthew suddenly slip from a skilled historian to a sloppy hack?

Not at all. He was applying the Israel narrative to Jesus' life because he wanted to show that Jesus, an Israelite himself, was reliving Israel's story. Central to that story was Moses, so Matthew made a point to highlight the unmistakable and remarkable parallels between Jesus and Moses.

They are many, but let's highlight seven of them.

Both escaped death at birth: Moses from Pharaoh in the Nile, Jesus from Herod in Bethlehem.

Both came out of Egypt: Moses with the Israelites, Jesus with his parents.

Both had a meaningful encounter with water: Moses with the parting of the Sea, Jesus with his baptism in the Jordan River.

Both entered the desert: Moses and Israel for forty years, Jesus for forty days.

Both led a group of twelve: Moses with the twelve tribes, Jesus with the twelve disciples.

Both ascended a mountain and expounded God's Word: Moses at Mount Sinai, Jesus at the Mount of Beatitudes.

Both revealed God in five movements: Moses recorded the first five books of the Bible (Genesis through Deuteronomy) known as the "Five Books of Moses." Matthew included five teaching blocks of Jesus in his gospel, beginning with the Sermon on the Mount.

Matthew clearly portrayed Jesus as the second Moses who was leading a new exodus. And Jesus, God's "Son," came from within Israel, God's "firstborn son." Jesus was reliving Israel's story to embody the mission God's people were meant to fulfill but couldn't.

With the words "Our Father," Jesus was announcing that freedom was on the way. That God is always the Rescuer. And that he always reaches for his children in love.

Some people listening to Jesus assumed he'd be delivering them from Roman rule, not knowing they needed deliverance from something far deeper and darker. A greater enemy still had to be dealt with. And as Jesus continued to teach the Lord's Prayer, he would point them to that reality.

THE FATHER WHO COMES RUNNING

Perhaps you're beginning to see God for the perfect parent he is. According to Henri Nouwen, the primary goal of Jesus' entire life was to reveal the "inexhaustible, unlimited motherly and fatherly love of his God and to show the way to let that love guide every part of our daily lives."[11]

If that's true, it changes everything about how we pray.

One of Jesus' most powerful stories about the nature of our Father God is often called the parable of the prodigal son (found in Luke 15). Jesus told this story while spending time with "tax collectors and sinners" (Luke 15:1)—which scandalized the religious leaders, who felt they were more deserving of Jesus' time and attention. In response, he told three stories about lost things: a sheep, a coin, and two sons. In each one, someone searches. In each one, something is found. And every time, there's a celebration. The last story about two lost sons is especially powerful.[12]

We hear about one son in rebellion and one in resentment, and their father reaches out to them both to absorb their heartache and make a way for them to come home.

It begins with the younger son publicly shaming his father by demanding his share of the inheritance before his father's death. His foolish and immature demand must have grieved the father's heart. And in an honor-shame culture, it also would have enraged the community.

Eventually the immature son realized the mess he'd made, but he knew the heart of his father. If he went home, his father would receive him back, even if only as a hired worker. So, knowing that his father was good, he began heading home.

Can you imagine that long, lonely walk? Shame pressing down with every step. He knew the village would see him coming. He knew the stares, the whispers, the snide comments about to be lobbed his way. He was already rehearsing what it would feel like when they hit the target of his self-loathing heart. So, he braced himself to walk a gauntlet of shame.

Except.

His father was watching.

And he saw. He felt. And he was concerned. So he came running.

God's fatherly love isn't confined to the past. The God who ran still comes running, because, like the perfect parent, he cannot resist the cries of his children.

I struggled to decode my children's cries and know what they truly needed when they were babies. But God already knows what we need. He's completely aware and full of compassion. Jesus put it best: "If you, then, though you are evil [i.e. you are a fallen and sinful human], know how to give good gifts to your children, how much more will your Father in heaven give good gifts to those who ask him!"(Matthew 7:11).

Maybe your image of God has been shaped more by absence than presence or more by abuse than care. If so, can you name those distorted images of God? Would you be willing to release them and receive the more compelling, more beautiful truth Jesus wants you to see?

What if, instead of merely knowing God is good, you actually experienced his goodness? What if you spoke the words "Our Father" not as a ritual, but as a return? A homecoming?

There was a time I simply believed that God was love. But now, I experience him as a Rescuer, crashing into my pain and lifting me from the things that hold me back. He wants the exact same thing for you, right now, with whatever pain you're holding or whatever barrier you're stuck against.

God is infinitely better than any human father you've ever known. He has none of their limitations, and more love to give than you could ever possibly imagine.

So when you pray, pray like this:

"Our Father . . ."

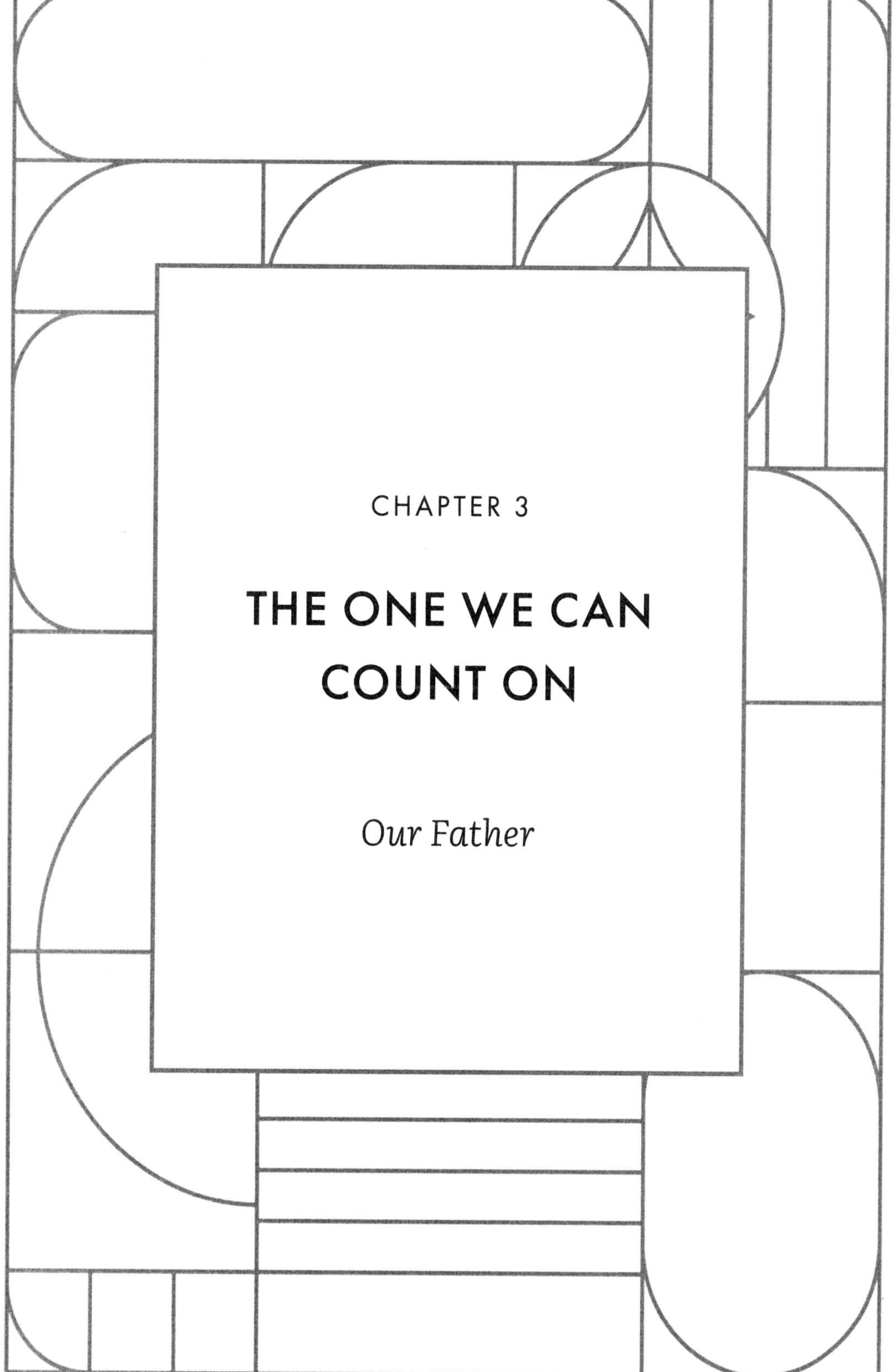

CHAPTER 3

THE ONE WE CAN COUNT ON

Our Father

BRAD NELSON

It's easy to believe God is a loving Father until things start blowing up. A marriage. A church. The life you thought you would live. The things you were so certain of.

In the last chapter, we explored the beauty of calling God *Father*—the one who sees, loves, and comes to rescue. But what happens when the rescue doesn't come? What do you do when, in the words of Andrew Peterson, you're "bleating for comfort from Thy staff and Thy rod, and heaven's only answer is the silence of God"?[1]

I remember the first time I heard that silence.

It was 2004. My brother-in-law Rich had just married my little sister. Their honeymoon was short since he deployed to Iraq soon after the wedding. I prayed for his safety more urgently and faithfully than I'd ever prayed for anything. Then, just weeks into his deployment, his Humvee was struck by a roadside bomb. He died instantly.

His death exposed my faith for the house of cards it really was. I never would have admitted it at the time, but in practice, I treated prayer like a cosmic gumball machine: Say the right words, believe hard enough, and out comes what you want. That kind of praying couldn't cut it after Rich died.

So I didn't pray. I *raged*. My prayers were honest, unfiltered, and devastating. One night, I lashed out: *I know you're near. I can feel your presence. Why won't you comfort me? Why are you just standing there watching me bleed out*? It was gut-wrenching. Not because God felt far away—but because he didn't. He was there. And still, it hurt.

Maybe you know that feeling.

Maybe you've prayed and lost. Trusted and still suffered. Sat in the wreckage, stunned and alone, unsure what to do next.

Maybe you've asked the question people of faith have been whispering for centuries: "What good is it to call God *Father* when he doesn't show up the way you hoped?"

You're not the first to ask.

BATTLE-TESTED TRUST

Picture a crowd gathered on the hillside, listening as Jesus taught them to pray, "Our Father." As we've said, these words were tied to the defiant hope that had sustained their ancestors throughout hundreds of years of exile, foreign oppression, and unfulfilled promises. After enduring a revolving door of pagan overlords—Egypt, Assyria, Babylon, Persia, and Greece—the Jewish people finally gained independence in 142 BC, twenty-five years after the Maccabean Revolt began. Finally, God was making good on the promise of a new exodus! But then, in 63 BC—eighty years later—the Romans arrived, and Israel once again fell under the rule of a foreign, pagan empire. How did they continue to trust that God was a Father who would rescue them?

I've met some extraordinary people who've suffered unimaginably. Occasionally, I'll catch myself thinking, *If anyone has the right to despair, it's them.* But again and again, they're the ones who radiate a quiet confidence and joy. It's like they've found a way to look pain and disappointment in the face and choose something stronger. Not naive optimism—the kind that insists things will get better—but a gritty, grounded hope.

That's the kind of hope the people standing on that hillside in first-century Galilee knew in their bones. Their trust in God wasn't naive. It was battle-tested, shaped and formed by their defining story, the exodus.

But here's the catch: It wasn't the rescue that taught them to trust. It was the wilderness, that vast, yawning space between Egypt and the promised land. The place where trust is ultimately forged.

Anthropologists have coined a word to describe this uncomfortable place: *liminal space*. Liminal space is the agonizing yet formative place where what *was* is no longer, and what *will be* has yet to take shape.

The years of infertility waiting for a baby.

The pit in your stomach as you wait on the results of the biopsy.

Excruciating seasons of financial insecurity wondering if or when you'll make it out the other side.

The crisis of faith occurs when our expectations and experience no longer align. In these moments, nothing matters more than knowing God as a Father who can be trusted.

Few have modeled this better than Jesus' Jewish ancestors. Their hope was forged through centuries of suffering, and their journey through liminal space offers us wisdom today. Their story can help us navigate our own "in-between spaces" and grow trust in the waiting.

Let's look closely at how they viewed delay as preparation and saw adversity as an invitation to intimacy.

DELAY AS PREPARATION

In the Bible, the number forty is deeply symbolic. As liturgical theologian Laurence Hull Stookey once explained, in Scripture the number forty represents "a span of time sufficient to accomplish what needs to take place."[2] It's a symbolic pattern that echoes through the story of God's people.

During the flood, it rained for forty days and nights. Moses' life unfolded in forty-year increments. Nineveh was given forty days to repent. Elijah fled to the wilderness for forty days. Jesus was in the desert for forty days. After his resurrection, "He appeared to them over a period of forty days and spoke about the kingdom of God" (Acts 1:3).

Whenever you see the number forty in the Bible—whether it's forty days or forty years—it's a clue that God was preparing something or someone for what was coming next.

More than once, the experience took place in the wilderness. At the time of the exodus, there was an ancient road running from Egypt to the land of Canaan. Egyptian documents referred to it as the Horus Road.[3] It's a legendary trade route that passed through the land of Canaan connecting Egypt to the rest of the world. Because of its strategic significance, Pharaoh had stationed military garrisons along the road, each a day's journey apart.

Scripture tells us, "When Pharaoh let the people go, God did not lead them on the road through the Philistine country [the Horus Road], though that was shorter. For God said, 'If they face war, they might change their minds and return to Egypt'" (Exodus 13:17).

So, God took them the long way—and by *long*, I mean *forty years.*

To Pharaoh, it looked like wandering. To the Israelites, it *felt* like wandering! But it wasn't senseless; it was strategic. God led them into the desert to honor their limitations but also to teach them to trust and depend on him.

Borrowing the words of Nelson Mandela, Rabbi Jonathan Sacks characterized Israel's forty years of wandering as "the long walk to freedom": "On the map, the distance from Egypt to the Promised Land is not far. But the message of Numbers is that it always takes longer than you think. For the journey is not just physical, a walk across the desert. It is psychological, moral, and spiritual. It takes as long as the time needed for human beings to change."[4]

Before they could enter the land, God needed to get the Egypt out of them.

Very often, before we can step into what God has for us, he first needs to address deep places within us. We're not told why, but the journey of trust frequently means allowing God to guide us through the very places we'd rather not go. And when we find ourselves in between, wondering, *What's taking so long?*, it's helpful to remember that, like a good Father, God uses liminal space to teach us the very skills we'll need for the future that awaits us.

In fact, the image of a parent preparing a child is exactly how the book of Deuteronomy frames Israel's wandering.

> Remember how the Lord your God led you all the way in the desert these forty years, to humble you and to test you in order to know what was in your heart, whether or not you would keep his commands. He humbled you, causing you to hunger and then feeding you with manna, which neither you nor your fathers had known, to teach you that man does not live on bread alone but on every word that comes from the mouth of the Lord. Your clothes did not wear out and your feet did not swell during these forty years. Know then in your heart that as a man disciplines his son, so the Lord your God disciplines you. (Deuteronomy 8:2–5)[5]

In essence, God was teaching his children the skills they would need for where he planned to take them next. And he did it by guiding them through an experience in which they'd have to learn to struggle well.

Has God ever taken you the long way? Have you ever caught yourself asking, "God, how many times am I going to have to learn this lesson before I get to move on to the next one?"

Several years ago, my wife stepped away from her career to stay home and raise our three daughters. While she's never once doubted it was the right choice, it was a decision that came at great personal cost, as it does for many parents. As our kids have gotten older, she's sensed God inviting her to bring her giftedness to some kind of meaningful work.

But stepping out and offering herself to the world in that way has brought deeply discouraging results. Over the last four years, she's pursued multiple certifications that haven't panned out. She's taken a few jobs, but they've all been entry-level positions, none of which have tapped into the depth of her ability. Despite her best efforts to be faithful and put herself out there, nothing has worked out (yet). When she talks about it, you can hear the futility and ache in her voice.

When we're in a season like this, it's tempting to think the way many of the Israelites must have and conclude, "I'm just wandering in circles!" But God is more committed to our character than our comfort. It sounds absurd, but it is in his kindness that he guides us on a long desert journey.

He wants our struggles to become our strengths and our pain to become our power.

Reflecting on one of the many periods of spiritual stagnation that marked his career as a pastor, Eugene Peterson wrote, "Didn't I know by now that growth, any growth—but especially character growth, spiritual growth, church growth, body-of-Christ growth, soul growth—had periods of spiritual dormancy?"[6] There will inevitably be seasons in our lives when it feels like nothing's happening. But, in that liminal space, "secret work has been done in us of which we've had no inkling."[7]

Part of the genius of the Lord's Prayer is that it summons us to resist the lie that "nothing's happening" by daily reminding ourselves of the truth that God is a loving Father who is leading us somewhere good. Even when we can't see it.

Despite her discouragement, my wife has written two simple phrases on a notecard and posted it where she'll see it every day. It reads, "I am not stuck. I am being prepared."

ADVERSITY AS INTIMACY

Preparation isn't the only thing that happens in the desert. Sometimes what God is building isn't just capacity, but closeness.

After forty years, the Israelites finally made it to the doorstep of Canaan, and in his final act as their leader, Moses delivered a farewell speech designed to remind them how close God had been to them in the wilderness. "In a desert land he found him [Israel], in a barren and howling waste. He shielded him and cared for him; he guarded him as the apple of his eye" (Deuteronomy 32:10).

Shielded.

Cared for.

Guarded.

Apple of his eye.

These are words of tenderness and intimacy.

"Apple of his eye" is a modern idiom expressing love and care, but in Hebrew, the meaning is much more visceral. *Ishon* means "little man in the eye."[8] The next time you're with family or a group of friends, find another person who's willing to try a Bible experiment with you. Stand facing each other so the tips of your noses are about four inches apart. If getting this close to another person's face feels a little much, that's the point. Now, look carefully into one another's eyes until you see your own reflection. In Hebrew, that's the little man in the eye.

Moses essentially told the people, "When you were in the wilderness, God was so close to you, he could look into your eyes and see his own reflection." Speaking on behalf of God, the prophet Jeremiah wrote, "I remember the devotion of your youth, how as a bride you loved me and followed me through the wilderness, through a land not sown" (Jeremiah 2:2).

For God, that closeness in the wilderness was like a honeymoon.

There are moments in our lives we'd never choose to live through again, moments we wouldn't wish on another person. Yet it's shocking how often we wouldn't trade them because of what they formed and shaped in us. People often remember these challenging seasons with dreamy eyes. "Remember when the church was just four families and a lunchroom? Those were the days!" Or, "Remember when it was just us in a six-hundred-square-foot apartment living off ramen? We didn't have much, but we had each other!"

In hindsight, we're able to look back on our wilderness experiences as sweet because they represent a closeness and intimacy that was born of dependence. Nothing brings us closer to God, closer to each other, and closer to our own true selves than the experience of pain.

Pastor Frederick Buechner once shared a particularly painful experience from his childhood at a conference, and afterward someone approached him. "You've had a lot of pain in your life, but you've been a good steward of it."

The stewardship of pain.

Those words haunted Buechner. After reflecting on them, he wrote,

> What does that mean? I think it means to keep in touch with your pain, to keep in touch with the sad times, with the hard times . . . because it is often those times when we were most alive, when we were somehow closest to being most vitally human beings. Keep in touch with it because it is at those moments of pain where you are most open to the pain of other people—most open to your own deep places. Keep in touch with those sad times because it is then that you are most aware of your own powerlessness . . . but also most aware of God's power to pull you through it, to be with you in it.[9]

To pray "Our Father" is to remember all the ways God was tender and close with us in the hard times, and to remember that adversity is always an invitation to intimacy.

CARRIED BY THE PRAYER

After my brother-in-law Rich died, the disappointment was so intense I nearly walked away from my faith. I remember thinking that either Karl Marx was right and religion is just the opium of the people, or I'd misunderstood this whole thing from the ground up.

At the time, I'd been reading a book by Rabbi Lawrence Kushner. In my grief, everything I turned to seemed hollow. But his words felt like a lifeline. So I found the phone number for his synagogue in California and left a message.

I never expected to hear back—but thirty minutes later, he called.

After hearing my story, he said, "You need a rabbi," and connected me with an old classmate of his named Albert Lewis—who, remarkably, lived in my town.

Over the next year, Rabbi Lewis guided me through the Jewish rituals of mourning: a sacred, structured framework for grief. The most surprising part for me was saying Kaddish, the mourner's prayer. Jewish children mourning a parent say Kaddish twice a day, every day, for a full year—but never alone. The prayer must be spoken aloud in the presence of ten others. And it says nothing about grief. It simply magnifies the character of God:

Magnified and sanctified
May His great Name be
In the world that He created,
As He wills,
And may His kingdom come
In your lives and in your days
And in the lives of all the house of Israel,
Swiftly and soon,
And say all Amen![10]

Sound familiar? Some scholars believe Jesus may have shaped the Lord's Prayer from the bones of Kaddish—transforming it into a prayer not just about God, but about how God's kingdom works itself out and into the lives of others through us.[11]

This realization changed the way I prayed. Each Thursday for the rest of the year, our small group would end our time together by lighting a candle, holding hands, and praying the Lord's Prayer. It was their way of saying, *Even if you can't believe these words right now, we'll believe them for you.*

On the one-year anniversary of Rich's death, I wrote them a letter, thanking each of them by name. And I realized God had, in fact, comforted me. Just not the way I'd expected.

His face looked like Steve and Chris.

Matt and Heather.

Mark and Carolyn.

Rick.

Bridgette.

Luke and Sarah.

Ryan and Jill.

Steve and Sarah.

And his face can look like yours, if you're willing to lean in and hold space for someone else's pain.

So when the bottom falls out and you find yourself praying, "Our Father . . ." through clenched teeth, wondering, *Where's the rescue?*—don't walk away. Don't check out or numb out. Reframe disappointment as an invitation to a deeper story. Because the wilderness isn't where God abandons you. It's where he forms you.

Pray these words, not because they feel true—but because they *are* true. And if you can't will yourself to mean them, surround yourself with people who can mean them for you. Let the words carry you until you can stand again.

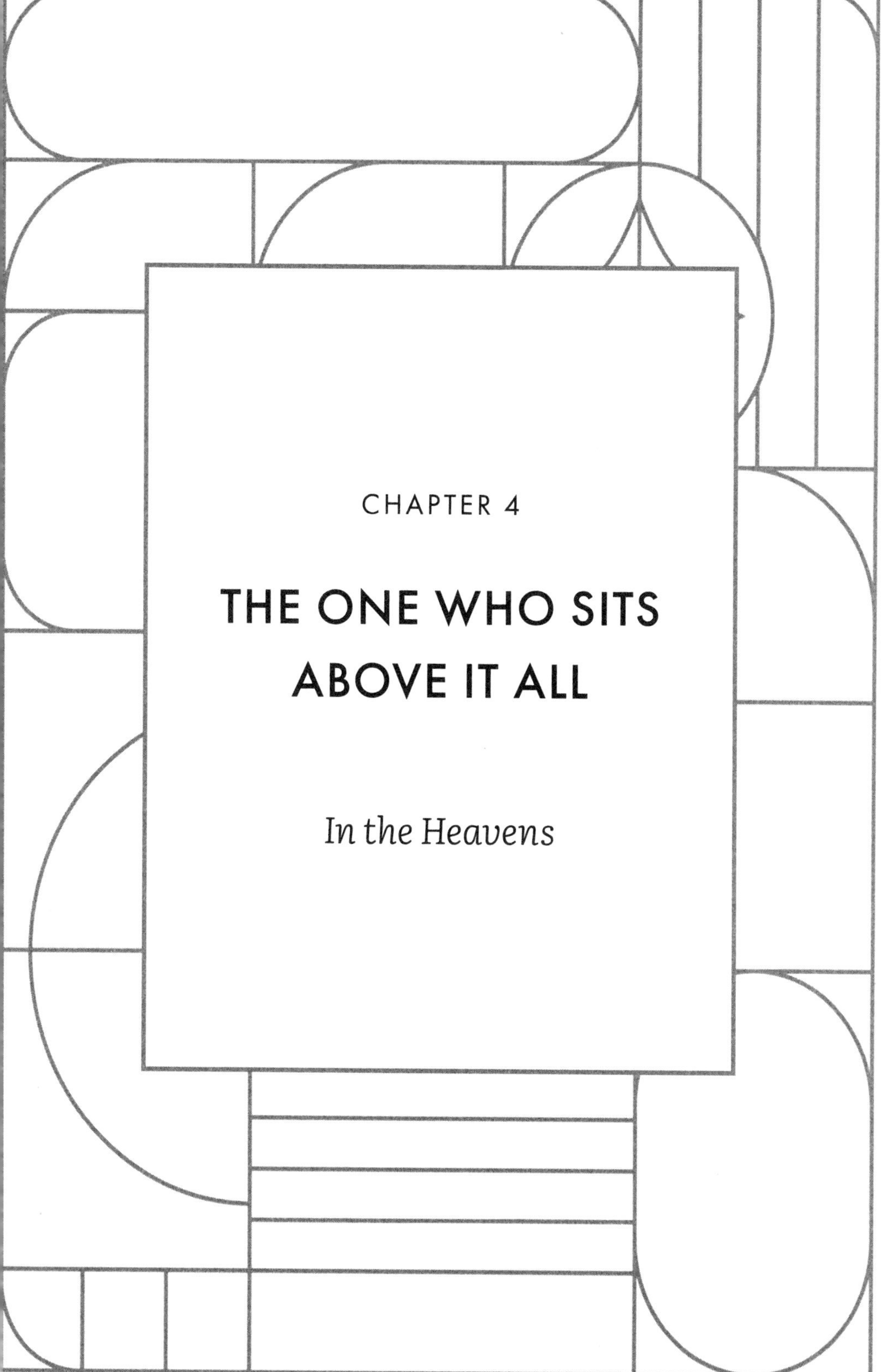

CHAPTER 4

THE ONE WHO SITS ABOVE IT ALL

In the Heavens

BRAD GRAY

I was a business management major in college, and my liberal arts program required me to take courses outside my field to "broaden my horizons." So, to check a box, I signed up for astronomy.

I thought I was just fulfilling a requirement. Little did I realize it would broaden my understanding of God's majesty and revolutionize my prayer life.

Like most college students, I was carrying a lot—questions about the future, pressure to succeed, a full calendar, and a gnawing uncertainty about where my life was headed. But when I started looking up at the stars, I discovered two things I didn't even know I was craving: a profound experience of awe and a much-needed shift in perspective.

Awe is what you feel when you stand in front of something so vast and beautiful, your brain can't compute—like standing on the edge of the Grand Canyon or the summit of a Swiss alpine mountain. All that bigness and beauty leaves you feeling small—but not insignificant. Awe has a way of shrinking our egos while expanding our souls. It reminds us we belong to something vast and alive, and somehow, we're part of it. That's what I felt studying the cosmos. I was thunderstruck by how enormous the universe is—and how strangely ordered.

David articulated something like this in Psalm 19:1–4: "The heavens declare the glory of God; the skies proclaim the work of his hands. Day after day they pour forth speech; night after night they reveal knowledge. They have no speech, they use no words; no sound is heard from them. Yet their voice goes out into all the earth, their words to the ends of the world."

According to astrophysicist Martin Rees, a mere six numbers

"constitute a recipe for the universe . . . if any one of them were to be 'untuned,' there would be no stars and no life."[1] The universe isn't random. It's breathtakingly precise. And ridiculously massive.

Here's a glimpse of what I was awakening to:

> Light travels at a blistering speed of 186,282 miles per second,[2] which is fast enough to circle Earth more than seven times in a single second. The moon is 240,000 miles away from Earth, so its light takes 1.3 seconds to reach us. The light from the sun, much farther away at 93 million miles, takes 8 minutes and 20 seconds to arrive here. Think about that the next time you're soaking up those rays! But here's where it gets really wild. The closest star to Earth (other than the sun) is Proxima Centauri. It takes light . . . wait for it . . . 4.2 years to get here! And that's our closest star![3]

Our galaxy, the Milky Way, is enormous—about 100,000 light-years across. So if you could hop on a beam of light and travel across the galaxy, it would take you 100,000 years to get from one end to the other—and that's traveling at 186,282 miles per second. To put that into perspective, since the moment Jesus gave the Lord's Prayer two thousand years ago, light has only traveled 1/50th of our galaxy!

That's a galactic mic drop right there.

And speaking of our galaxy, the Milky Way is packed with stars, somewhere between 150 and 200 billion of them.[4] The Virgo galaxy is estimated to have 5 trillion stars all to itself.[5] And these are just two of the estimated 200 billion galaxies in our universe.[6]

This brings a whole new context to Psalm 147, which says God "determines the number of stars and calls them each by name. Great is our Lord and mighty in power; his understanding has no limit" (vv. 4–5).

We live in an astonishing universe! And somehow the God who flung those stars into space isn't just powerful; he's also personal.

As we reflect on his wonders, we can say with the psalmist, "When I consider your heavens, the work of your fingers, the moon and the stars, which you have set in place, what is mankind that you are mindful of them, human beings that you care for them? You have made them a little lower than the angels and crowned them with glory and honor" (Psalm 8:3–5).

That's the paradox of awe. It makes us feel small but never unseen. For me, that realization changed everything. The sheer scale and precision of the universe did more than stir wonder—it stirred trust. If God is big enough to hold all this together, then surely he's big enough to hold me together too. That thought began to reshape how I saw my life, how I prayed, and how I walked with God in seasons of uncertainty. The stars were witnesses to a presence I could rely on.

REORIENTING THE HEART

That feeling of awe—the inner stillness that captivates you in the face of something vast and beautiful—isn't just emotional. It's spiritual. Rabbi Abraham Joshua Heschel wrote, "Awe is a sense for the transcendence, for the reference everywhere to the mystery beyond all things. It enables us to perceive in the world intimations of the Divine."[7]

Heschel understood that awe does more than make us feel small. It helps us perceive that which is beyond and behind and beneath all things—and connects us more deeply to the one who holds it all together. I don't know about you, but that's the kind of perspective I desperately need, because let's be honest: Life doesn't always feel like it's being held together by a wisdom and power from beyond.

Instead, it usually resembles a relentless game of Whac-A-Mole—deadlines, setbacks, and fires to put out. We read the news and feel a shudder deep inside. A text message turns our world upside down. Global crises, personal disappointments, and the confusion about where any of this is headed make it feel like life is unraveling, like we're hurtling headlong toward apocalyptic doom, not a new creation.

When that sense of unraveling takes over, it awakens all our worst instincts: fear, anxiety, control, fight-or-flight, and self-preservation. In those moments, we wonder, *Is anyone really in control?*

Consider this for a moment, though: What if that very sense of overwhelm could serve as a signal? What if it's not evidence that God is absent—but an invitation to elevate our perspective?

That's what Jesus invites us into every day when we pray, "Our Father in heaven . . ." Saying those words helps us shift our focus—not just to *who* God is, but to *where* God is. Not geographically, but cosmically. He's enthroned in heaven: above the chaos, beyond the noise. He sees what we can't. He rules with wisdom and perspective we don't have. And he holds together what feels like it's falling apart.

As God himself declared, "As the heavens are higher than the earth, so are my ways higher than your ways and my thoughts than your thoughts" (Isaiah 55:9).

So when life feels unstable, "Our Father in heaven" becomes a kind of spiritual overview, an invitation to reorient our hearts by lifting our eyes to the one who stretched out the galaxies and still knows us by name.

ENVISIONING HEAVEN

What images come to mind when you hear that God the Father is *in heaven*? Maybe it's a staircase into the clouds or a distant throne in the sky. We might have a vague notion of "the man upstairs" or think of athletes celebrating with prayerful gestures to the sky. Heaven, we assume, is somewhere up there.

Back in the 1980s, my biblical imagination was forged by a cutting-edge presentation tool called the *flannelgraph*. On this flannel board with movable cutouts, God was depicted as an old man with a white beard seated on a throne of clouds. Around him, people on other clouds wore white robes and joyously sang hymns for all eternity. The flannelgraph indicated that heaven was a place people went after they died. So it was a place far away that you only could reach later.

That kind of imagery isn't just outdated; it's incomplete.

If heaven is merely a distant, postmortem holding place, God appears to be removed from our daily reality. If that's how we think about heaven, we can easily assume God is disinterested in our lives. This kind of theology distorts our perception of God, as Dallas Willard once explained: "The damage done to our practical faith in Christ . . . by confusing heaven with a place in distant or outer space, or even beyond space, is incalculable."[8]

While the New Testament teaches that Christians will be with Jesus in heaven after they die, heaven has a much more significant role in the biblical story, and it's meant to have a much more significant role in our daily lives. To see why heaven matters—not just after we die but right now—we need to understand what "Our Father in heaven" would've meant to Jesus' first listeners. Their vision of who God is and where he dwells came from an ancient way of seeing the world that's very different from ours.

We have to recover their ancient imagination, because when we do, we'll find it won't just change how we pray; it will reshape how we see reality itself.

ANCIENT COSMOLOGY

In the ancient world, people understood the universe from the ground up—literally. Without telescopes or satellite imagery, their view of the cosmos was shaped entirely by what they could see: the earth beneath their feet and the heavens above their heads. And that's how they divided their world: the heavens and the earth.

Which is exactly how Genesis begins: "In the beginning, God created the heavens and the earth."

The Hebrew word for "heavens" is *shamayim*, a plural term. Interestingly, the Greek word translated as "heaven" in the opening of the Lord's Prayer is *ouranois*—also plural. So in the original Greek of Matthew 6:9, Jesus says, "Our Father in the heavens."

Yet most of us grew up saying, "Our Father in heaven."

This isn't wrong—it's just incomplete. Recovering the Israelite view of the cosmos deepens our understanding of where our Father is—and what Jesus was emphasizing in this part of the prayer.

In the ancient imagination, the heavens weren't a single, undifferentiated space. They were layered, divided into three distinct levels:

Level one was the sky above (the atmosphere) where birds fly and clouds roll by.

Level two was the realm of the sun, moon, and stars (what we call outer space). The ancients believed these celestial lights were fixed to a vast dome—a vaulted expanse described in Genesis 1:6, often referred to as the firmament.

Level three lay beyond the visible dome. Known as the "heaven of heavens" or the "highest heavens," it was understood as the transcendent realm where God dwells—enthroned above all powers, rulers, and realms. It's from here that God rules and reigns, judges and loves, all that he has created.[9]

Even a basic grasp of this layered cosmos brings clarity to many biblical texts.

Psalm 113 declares, "The LORD is exalted over all the nations, his glory above the heavens. Who is like the LORD our God, the One who sits enthroned on high, who stoops down to look on the heavens and the earth?" (vv. 4–6).

Psalm 115:16 states, "The highest heavens belong to the LORD, but the earth he has given to mankind." While the entire cosmos belongs to God, this verse highlights the distinction between God's dwelling place and humanity's—and how they function differently.

In Psalm 123, we read that God is "enthroned in the heavens" (v. 1 NRSV).

The book of Job describes God walking on "the vaulted heavens" (22:14).

And during Solomon's temple dedication prayer, he marvels, "But will God really dwell on earth? The heavens, even the highest heaven, cannot contain you. How much less this temple I have built!" (1 Kings 8:27).

In the New Testament, 2 Corinthians 12:2 recounts Paul's vision of being "caught up to the third heaven"—meaning, into God's very presence. This layered view of the cosmos was so familiar to his audience that Paul didn't feel the need to explain it.[10]

So when Jesus teaches us to pray, "Our Father in the heavens," he's reminding us: God reigns. Not from a distant place of disinterest, but from the highest place of authority—where his will is perfectly done and peace already reigns.

Which, of course, is quite different from what we experience here on earth. There's a tension—between the chaos below and the shalom above. And later in the Lord's Prayer, we'll see how God intends to resolve that tension.

REIGNING AND LOVING

When Jesus began the prayer with "Our Father *in the heavens*," he was reminding his listeners that the one who loved them was also the one who reigns above it all, and in a polytheistic world, that was a bold and exclusive claim.

The ancients believed in many gods, each ruling over their own territory. Although the Bible acknowledges the existence of other divine beings, it always places them in a subservient role to the God of the cosmos.

For example, in the book of Exodus, God declared, "I will bring judgment on all the gods of Egypt" (12:12).

Once the Israelites were safely out of the reach of Pharaoh, they sang, "Who among the gods is like you, Lord?" (Exodus 15:11).

Even Psalm 82 critiques lesser divine beings who misuse their power, saying, "You are 'gods'; you are all sons of the Most High. But you will die like mere mortals; you will fall like every other ruler" (vv. 6–7).

So with the words "Our Father in the heavens," Jesus was telling his ancient listeners: *The one who sees you, knows you, and cares for you is also the one who reigns over every dimension of the cosmos. He has no equal. Not Baal. Not Zeus. Not Caesar.*

That's what gives this prayer its power.

Saying "Our Father in the heavens" means centering your life on the one who not only flung the stars into space but also knows each one by name (Psalm 147:4)—and he knows yours too.

THE (SPIRITUAL) OVERVIEW EFFECT

Right about now, some of you are probably thinking, *That's all well and good, but I don't wake up thinking about cosmology and grammar.*

True. We wake up thinking about more pressing things: bills that need to be paid, relationships that need mending, the stress of a to-do list we can barely keep up with. And that's exactly why Jesus invites us to anchor our souls, on a daily basis, in the reality that our Father is *in the heavens.*

In the late 1980s, author and space philosopher (now there's a job title!) Frank White coined the term "the overview effect" to describe the shift in worldview reported among American astronauts and Russian cosmonauts during spaceflight. Apparently, seeing our world from the vantage point of space has a profound impact on the human psyche.

According to White, "the experience often transforms astronauts' perspective on the planet and humanity's place in the universe."[11] He described how astronauts often returned to earth with a radically different perspective, a profound sense that everything is interconnected, and a deeper desire to care for our world.

That's what the Lord's Prayer gives us—a spiritual overview. When we acquire the habit of zooming out and seeing things from a divine perspective, we're reminded that this whole thing is headed somewhere good.

But God's care isn't just cosmic. In the eyes of our Creator, *we matter.*

As Jesus put it, "Are not two sparrows sold for a penny? Yet not one of them will fall to the ground apart from the will of your Father. And even the very hairs of your head are all numbered. So don't be afraid; you are worth more than many sparrows" (Matthew 10:29–31).[12]

In other words, our Father in the heavens sees the intricate details of our lives, and that makes all the difference in seasons of uncertainty.

When we set out to film season one of *The Sacred Thread*, we knew it would be a massive undertaking—creating seven episodes connected to the Lord's Prayer filmed across multiple countries. But we couldn't have guessed the extensive challenges it would involve.

One of the countries kept closing the door to us—even though we had filmed there before without issue. We followed every protocol, submitted the proper paperwork, and exhausted every possible connection—and still the permission never came.

Throughout that draining, confusing, sometimes heartbreaking season, I found myself praying, *God, why now? Why this? You called us to this work. You've carried us through so much. Why leave us hanging here, so close to the finish line?*

In moments like these the phrase "Our Father in the heavens" anchors me. Because if God really is in the heavens—if he sees what I can't, knows what I don't, and holds the whole story together—this closed door isn't the end. It's just part of the story I don't understand yet.

He's the one who created the cosmos and sustains every atom. He's not lost. He's not late. He's not unaware.

Maybe you're in a similar place right now—staring at a closed door, stuck in a waiting season, carrying questions that have no answers. If so, here's what I invite you to do: Take a break, step outside, and look up. Let the night sky remind you that you're not alone. Let the stars preach to you. Our Father is in the heavens. He's above it all—and with you in it all. He sees. He knows. He's got this.

And you can trust him—even here.

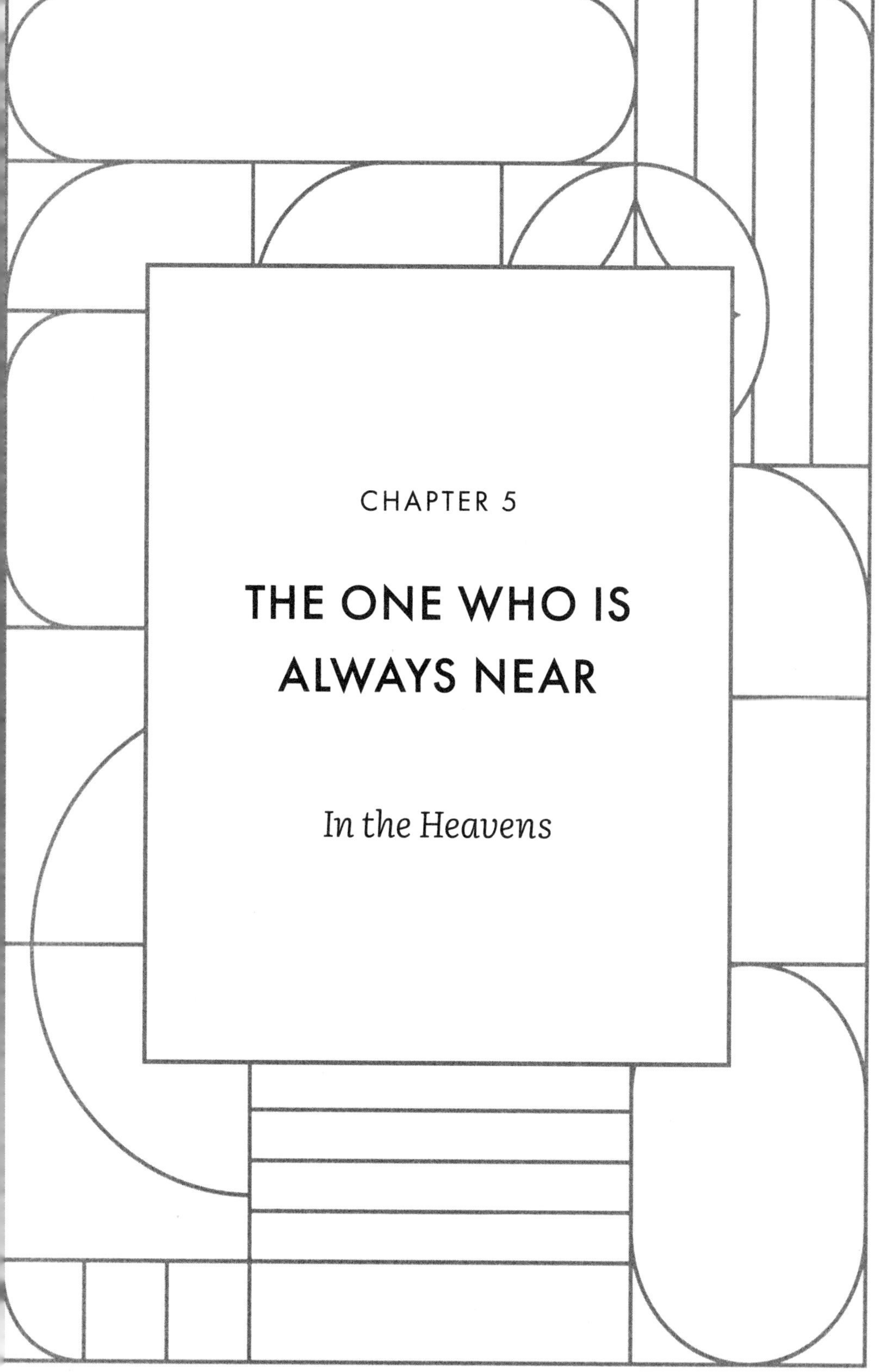

CHAPTER 5

THE ONE WHO IS ALWAYS NEAR

In the Heavens

BRAD NELSON

There are moments in life that stop us in our tracks and linger in our memories for years. They seem to connect us to what feels like a larger, truer, and deeper dimension of reality. I'm not talking about milestone moments like graduating from school, getting married, or beating cancer. Those are noteworthy for obvious reasons. What I'm talking about are the little, unexpected ones that somehow meet our deepest longings and wildest hopes.

In his book *The Second Mountain*, David Brooks described one such moment in his life:

> I came home from work one summer evening and pulled into the driveway on the side of the house and found my three kids, then twelve, nine, and four, playing with a plastic ball in the backyard. They were kicking it in the air and then racing one another across the grass to catch it. They were giggling and tumbling all over one another and having a deliriously good time. I sat there in the car looking at this tableau of family happiness through the windshield. The summer sun glowed through the trees. My lawn, for some reason, looked perfect. I experienced a sort of liquid joy and overflowing gratitude that seemed to stop time, that made my heart swell.[1]

When have you had a version of this sort of moment?

It's a time when the clouds part, the veil is lifted, and for a split second, you see life the way God intended it to be. Life at its purest and best.

These sightings share three characteristics: They're ordinary, profound, and fleeting. They happen when you're simply going about your day—and then *bam*, you catch a glimpse of something profound. You feel gratitude and joy begin to well up, and, before you know it, it's gone.

Beauty does this to us. A sunset can turn a stretch of road you've driven a hundred times into an enchanting and otherworldly place, and before you know what you're doing, you're whispering, "Thank you."

Sometimes it happens in the context of relationships. Have you ever shared a meal or conversation with someone that was so charged with holiness that it left you wondering, *What was* that? Or maybe someone spoke the words you needed to hear at the exact moment you needed to hear them.

I'm convinced these moments move us the way they do because they're a glimpse of the life we were made for—a taste of heaven and earth coming together.

And this, I believe, is exactly what Jesus had in mind when he taught us to pray to "Our Father in the heavens." He wasn't giving us a formula; he was offering a lens. A way of seeing. A daily practice for reorienting our attention to the God who's not distant—but present. A Father whose presence seeps into our world like light through a cracked door, visible only to those awake enough to perceive it.

When Jesus invites us to pray this way, he's also inviting us to live this way. With eyes wide open. With hearts tuned to the sacred. With an awareness that heaven isn't just a future reality but a dimension of our everyday lives. Revelation 21:1–3 tells us that one day heaven and earth will be reunited, and as we live in anticipation of that future, we're not meant to wait with folded hands. We're called to anticipate it by cultivating a life of conscious awareness of the many ways heaven is breaking in here—and joining God in making it visible.

But not everyone sees the world this way.

Sometimes, when we zoom out to take in the big picture, we don't feel wonder. We feel dread.

When NASA's *Apollo 17* mission captured the first photograph of

Earth from deep space in 1972, people around the globe marveled at the fragile beauty of our planet suspended in black. But not everyone saw hope in that image.

Reflecting on that "pale blue dot," astronomer Carl Sagan wrote, "Our planet is a lonely speck in the great enveloping cosmic dark. In our obscurity, in all this vastness, there is no hint that help will come from elsewhere to save us from ourselves."[2]

Sagan gave voice to a fear many of us carry just beneath the surface: *What if we're on our own? What if no one's coming to save us? What if none of this matters?* That ache lives underneath our longing for those small, luminous moments. We want to believe our lives are more than just a happy accident in an indifferent universe. That there is meaning here.

Jesus speaks directly to that longing with the words, "Our Father *in the heavens*" (Matthew 6:9, emphasis added). In just five words, he reframes the cosmos. He names a God who is not only sovereign over all things but present in all things. A God whose nearness can transform even the most ordinary moment into holy ground.

But to fully appreciate how disruptive—and how hopeful—those words truly are, we need to revisit the ancient understanding of the heavens—this time, through the lens of how people related to the gods who were believed to dwell there.

DISTANT AND DETACHED

In the ancient world, no one doubted that the gods existed. People simply assumed they were responsible for everything that happened on earth. If your crops failed, your kid got sick, or your army lost a battle, the explanation was obvious: The gods were angry. The Romans called it the *pax deorum*—the peace of the gods—and they were careful not to disturb it.

Historian Thomas Cahill described the Greek gods as "human beings made gigantic, as full of needs as of power and requiring the stateliness of ritual—soothing actions performed the same way over and over again—in order to be assuaged. Such actions always require loss for men and gain for the gods."[3]

But not all ancient people imagined the gods as cruel or detached. There are traces of hope, even tenderness, in some traditions. Some believed their gods capable of compassion, empathy, and protection. Still, even among the more hopeful, the relationship was mostly transactional. You performed the right ritual, in the right way, at the right place and time. And if you didn't? You might bring down divine wrath.

Roman religion, for example, had to be executed with absolute precision. The slightest procedural mistake could invalidate entire rituals, or, worse, offend the gods.

In many ancient cultures, the heavens were associated with the divine dwelling place of the gods. Getting their attention meant going up, so people viewed mountains as the meeting place between heaven and earth. They built outdoor sanctuaries on mountaintops or massive structures like ziggurats and pyramids, shaping them to resemble mountains bridging heaven and earth.[4] Likewise, a god's temple on earth was thought to mirror that god's temple in the heavens.

These were the places ancient people offered sacrifices to the gods. If their sacrifices didn't work, they'd double down, offering something more valuable. Eventually, some rationalized sacrificing what was most precious—their children.

Tragically, even God's own people weren't immune to this. Both King Ahaz and King Manasseh sacrificed children to the Ammonite god Molek in the Hinnom Valley in Jerusalem (2 Kings 16:3, 21:6). Following their example, the common people did as well (23:10).

To be clear, they sacrificed their children to a pagan god. The God of the Bible was outraged by this: "They built high places for Baal in the Valley of Ben Hinnom to sacrifice their sons and daughters to Molek, though I never commanded, nor did it enter my mind, that they should do such a detestable thing and so make Judah sin" (Jeremiah 32:35).

This was a problem with ancient sacrificial systems: They left people wondering, *When is* enough, *enough?* An Akkadian prayer known as the

"Prayer to Any God," written around the same time as the exodus, captures the helplessness of trying to satisfy the gods:

May (my) lord's angry heart be reconciled,
May the god I do not know be reconciled,
May the goddess I do not know be reconciled,
May the god, whoever he is, be reconciled,
May the goddess, whoever she is, be reconciled . . .
O god, whoever you are, many are my wrongs, great my sins,
O goddess, whoever you are, many are my wrongs, great my sins!
I do not know what wrong I have done,
I do not know what sin I have committed,
I do not know what abomination I have perpetrated,
I do not know what taboo I have violated![5]

You can feel the desperation in those words. This is prayer as groping in the dark, pleading for someone—anyone—to notice, to care, to help.

But that's not how the sacrificial system of Jesus' ancestors worked.

In the book of Leviticus, God gave Israel a radically different framework. He spelled out in painstaking detail exactly what sacrifices to offer and when. No guessing. No offering more and more in the hopes of finally getting God's attention. And absolutely no child sacrifice!

In doing so, God was offering his people something unthinkable: a way for his holy presence to come down, be known, and dwell among his people.

MOMENTS WE DON'T WANT TO MISS

The Bible is filled with stories of God moving through the heavens and drawing near to his people in the most unexpected places.[6]

When Jacob was on the run after stealing his brother Esau's blessing, he rested for the night at Bethel. While sleeping, he dreamed of a ladder reaching up to the heavens and saw God above the ladder. When he awoke, he was awestruck. God was there with him! "This is none other than the house of God; this is the gate of heaven" (Genesis 28:17).

Several details make this story stand out. First, Jacob wasn't at a high place or a temple—places Ancient Near Eastern people would expect heaven and the earth to overlap. Second, he wasn't even looking for God. Then, suddenly, the God of the heavens appeared to him *in the middle of nowhere.*

God didn't wait for Jacob to climb up; God came down to him.

Praying "Our Father in the heavens" invites us to live with the conviction that the heavenly, unseen realm is as real and present as the air we breathe—that every place can become holy ground if only we have eyes to see it. So even the phrase "Our Father in the heavens" can remind us that our Father is always near us.[7]

What David Brooks saw while watching his kids play, and what each of us sees in our own heavenly moments, is the house of God, the gate of the heavens. These moments awaken us to the fact that God is in that place! And the more we pray this way, the more we'll live this way.

Unfortunately, these little glimpses of heaven and earth coming together are the exception, not the rule. Most of the time, we're just going through the motions: sending emails, getting kids to school, scrolling on our phones. Unless we cultivate a conscious awareness of heaven's availability right here, right now, the current of modern life will lull us to sleep, rendering us oblivious to the heavens on offer all around us. When that happens, we start missing the moments—not because God is absent but because we are.

One of my favorite Jewish tales is about two Israelites, Reuven and Shimon, and what happened to them when God miraculously parted the waters of the Red Sea. Recounting the story in his book *God Was in This Place and I, I Did Not Know,* Rabbi Lawrence Kushner wrote,

> Apparently the bottom of the sea, though safe to walk on, was not completely dry but a little muddy, like a beach at low tide.

Reuven stepped into it and curled his lip. "What is this muck?"

Shimon scowled, "There's mud all over the place!"

"This is just like the slime pits of Egypt!" replied Reuven.

"What's the difference?" complained Shimon. "Mud here, mud there; it's all the same."

And so it went for the two of them, grumbling all the way across the bottom of the sea. And, because they never once looked up, they never understood why on the distant shore everyone else was singing songs of praise. For Reuven and Shimon the miracle never happened.[8]

How often are we oblivious to God's intervention in our daily lives because, like Reuven and Shimon, our attention is focused elsewhere?

How do we wake up? How do we resist the gravitational pull toward spiritual sleepwalking and live more consciously aware of the heavens all around us?

CHOOSING TO BE FULLY PRESENT

God knows we are wired to need guidance here.

He once instructed Moses to meet with him on Mount Sinai, which would have meant a grueling hike up to an elevation of more than seven thousand feet.[9] Picture him doubled over with his hands on his knees sucking wind. By the time he reached the top, he was probably exhausted and wondering, *How long will it take to get back down?*

Knowing that human beings possess a deeply ingrained tendency to be anywhere but the present moment, God told Moses beforehand, "Come up to me on the mountain and stay here" (Exodus 24:12). The last phrase comes from the Hebrew *hayah*, which can mean "to stay or to be."[10] So God was essentially saying, "When you get here, *be here*. I need you to be fully present."

We've all experienced people who aren't fully present. They're there but not there. They're fiddling with their phone, their gaze keeps drifting to the screen on the wall behind you, or their blank expression tells you their thoughts are elsewhere. Sometimes all it takes is one look at my wife's face to know her sponge is full and my story needs to wait. We've got a sixth sense for knowing when people are with us and when they're not.

The only thing worse than talking to someone who's not fully present is being the one who's not fully present. A few weeks ago, my eight-year-old brought home a drawing she made in her second-grade art class. It was a sketch of me watching soccer highlights on my phone.

On the other hand, you know when you're with someone who's fully present. Their attention has an unmistakable quality and generosity to it. They're unhurried. They look you in the eye. They ask thoughtful questions. Their presence leaves you feeling seen, heard, and known.

People who are fully present can even have an unnerving effect on you. They recognize when you're off. When they listen to you, they're able to hear the thing behind the thing. It can even feel like they've been reading your mail.

Jesus had this sort of impact on people.

In Luke 8, he demonstrated profound awareness of a particular woman amid a chaotic crowd. For twelve years she'd been suffering a bleeding condition, but when she touched his cloak from behind him, she was immediately healed.

Despite being nearly crushed by the people around him, Jesus sensed something had changed.

"Who touched me?" Jesus asked.

Pointing out the obvious, Peter replied, "The people are crowding and pressing against you." *Uh, Jesus. Everyone's touching you.*

Then Jesus clarified his meaning: "I know that power has gone out from me" (Luke 8:46).

Trembling, the woman fell at his feet and explained what had happened.

People simply could not go unnoticed in Jesus' presence. He was always dialed in to what the Spirit was doing in the moment, what his

Father wanted, and what was happening in the people around him. He exemplified living the eternal kind of life *now*.

Jesus lived fully present to the heavens breaking in all around him, and he invites us to live the same way. But that kind of attentiveness doesn't come naturally. In a world of noise and hurry, it must be cultivated.

And the way we cultivate it is through prayer.

Not prayer as routine or obligation, but prayer as the daily practice of directing our attention. A way of reorienting ourselves toward what matters most.

PRAYER AS ATTENTION

It's impossible to experience the eternal kind of life apart from prayer, because prayer is the way we direct our attention to God. As Simone Weil said, "Absolutely unmixed attention is prayer."[11]

A million things fight for our attention on a daily basis. Smartphones, social media, and constant connection dominate our focus; every notification and nudge seeks to pull us out of the present moment to some other place. As author Wendell Berry observed, we are "subjected almost from the cradle to an overwhelming insinuation that all worth experiencing is somewhere else."[12]

We move through life at a breathless pace, skimming the surface of our days but rarely sinking into the present moment. We pack our schedules to the brim. We run a side hustle. Our kids play travel sports. We convince ourselves it's just a season, but the finish line keeps moving. What begins as, "If I can just get through Wednesday," becomes, "I'll be able to catch my breath after Christmas." But busyness is no longer a season; it's a way of life, one that slowly numbs our capacity to notice what matters most.

We even "busy brag," signaling that we're important. We're in demand. We're getting things done. In a speech delivered at the World

Economic Forum in 2009, Desmond Tutu joked that in our culture of achievement "stomach ulcers become status symbols."[13]

Being fully present to the kingdom of the heavens in the here and now through a life of prayer is simply not compatible with a life of compulsive busyness. Our attention is a precious and powerful resource, and what we do with it determines, in large part, the kind of people we become.

And that's just it—beholding takes practice. If we don't learn it, we don't just miss the moments, we miss the God showing up in them. Constant distraction doesn't just scatter our attention; it spiritually deforms us. Discipled into distraction, we become half present at best: half present to the people we love, and half awake to the God we serve. I can't think of anything more heartbreaking than realizing I missed a sacred moment—one that could've drawn me closer to God or others—because I was watching a reel, or replying to a text, or—God help me—I was too busy.

I wish I could tell you I've cracked the code, but more often than not, I'm like Reuven and Shimon—so focused on the mud that I miss the miracle. But when you cultivate a life of presence, the Lord's Prayer primes you to spot those moments when, like Jacob, you trip over the gate of heaven.

One of those moments found me at the end of my driveway, in an old chair, with my little girl.

When I graduated from college, my parents gave me a La-Z-Boy recliner. I loved that chair. It followed us from apartment to home, and across the country from Michigan to Florida. Over time, it acquired the telltale signs of family life—stains, torn fabric, and a Sharpie incident courtesy of one of the kids. Eventually it was exiled from the living room and reassigned to nursery duty. That chair rocked all three of our daughters to sleep.

But it was huge. Obnoxiously huge. One night, while my wife Trisha and the girls were out, I decided it was time. I hauled it down to the end of the driveway and taped a FREE sign to the front.

When they got home and our youngest, Charlotte, saw it, she froze.

Her eyes welled up with tears. That chair wasn't just a piece of furniture. It was a piece of her childhood. Her grief caught me off guard.

So I picked her up and said, "What if we say goodbye with one last rock before bed?"

She nodded.

By then, the stars were out, and as we sat at the end of the driveway—her head on my chest, thumb in her mouth, and the old chair quietly squeaking beneath us—we whispered a prayer of thanks for all the stories it held and all the nights it rocked us home.

And for several moments, everything was still.

No agenda. No hurry. Just presence. Just me and my little girl, saying goodbye to a chair.

It was just a chair at the end of the driveway, but for a moment, it became holy ground.

That's what this prayer does. It trains us to see the holy in the ordinary. It opens our eyes and hearts to the God who is close, and it reminds us that heaven isn't far off—it's right here, in the rocking chair, in the driveway, in the now. But only if we're awake to it.

Don't let the pace of life steal your attention. Refuse to be discipled into distraction. Take back your attention by consciously directing it to "Our Father in the heavens." Begin each day with these words. Then pause, looking back over the previous twenty-four hours. Where did God draw near? Choose to consciously savor those moments of closeness, knowing that the more you do, the more you'll be capable of seeing tomorrow. Who knows where the next crack of light will shine through?

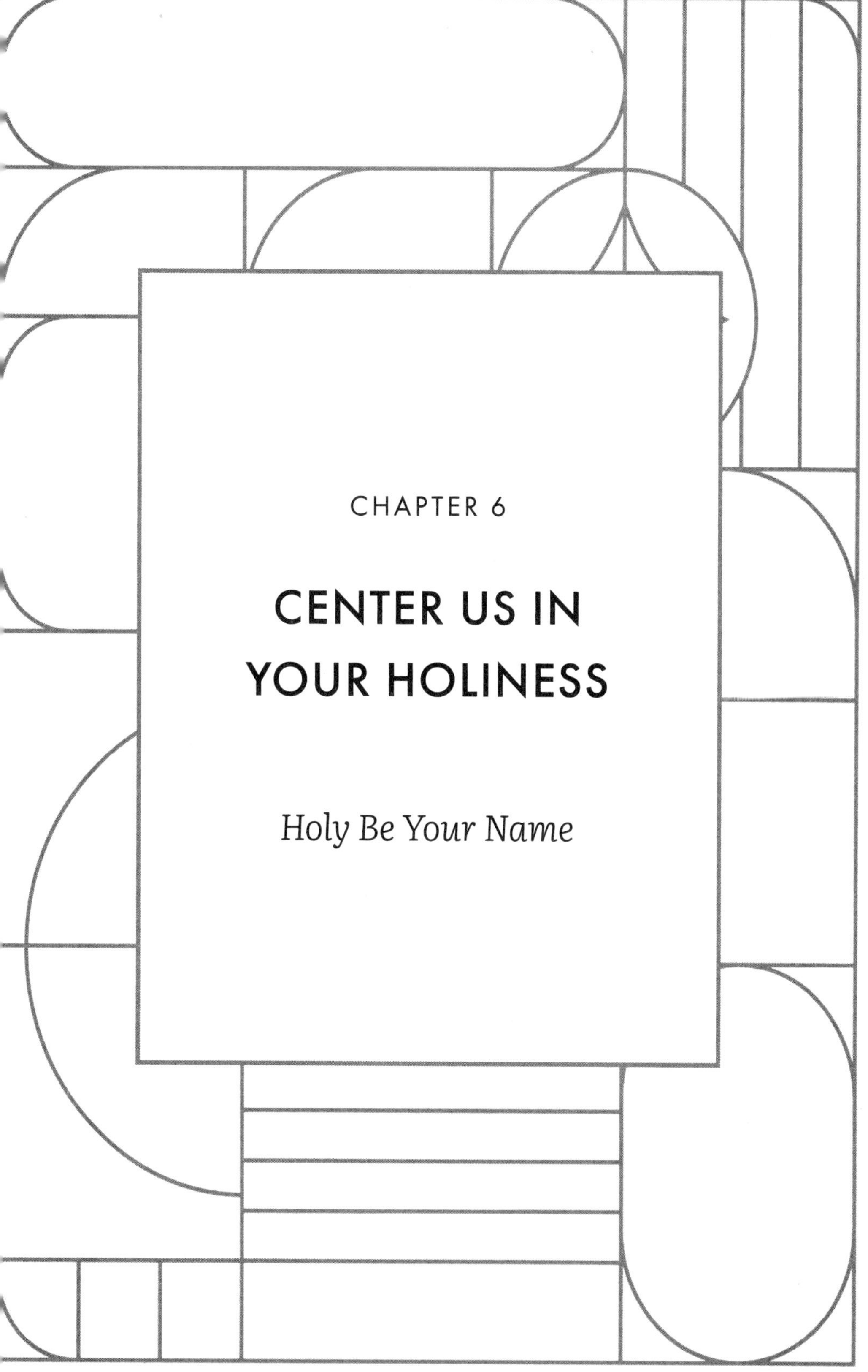

CHAPTER 6

CENTER US IN YOUR HOLINESS

Holy Be Your Name

BRAD NELSON

I recently read an article about a rare shark attack off the coast of Israel. It happened near a power plant that pumps warm water into the sea, creating an unusual ecosystem teeming with sharks. The article showed a photo of seven beachgoers, standing in waist-deep water, filming a ten-foot shark swimming just yards away.[1]

Maybe it's because I watched *Jaws* as a ten-year-old, or because I suffer from a little thing called common sense, but I said out loud, "That's a bad idea."

You can picture the scene: laughter, nervous chatter, people fumbling for their phones to capture the moment. Captivated by the majesty of this creature, they couldn't stop watching.

But in their fascination, they forgot their fear.

I see this sort of thing online all the time. A tourist in Yellowstone gets too close to a bison. A visitor to Canada poses foolishly beside a moose. Someone falls off a cliff trying to get the perfect selfie.

I get the impulse. Beauty and majesty have a way of pulling us in. But if we're not careful, we lose an appropriate sense of danger. We forget how high that cliff is or how that wild creature could turn and flatten us in an instant. When we fail to balance our fascination with an appropriate fear, we put ourselves in danger.

And strangely enough, something similar can happen in our relationship with God.

In our effort to draw near, we sometimes become casual in that nearness—flippant, even.

Compelled by his goodness, his nearness, and his love, we sometimes forget his holiness. If we approach him too casually or flippantly, we run the risk of domesticating the divine, caging the lion, and making God in our own image. When that happens, we end up with a mascot, not a Master, and then wonder why our faith feels shallow and lacking.

Years ago, I attended a conference where N. T. Wright was speaking. Before he took the stage, the room pulsated with music, lights, a fog machine, and vivid visuals; it was an immersive experience designed to stir the heart.

When the spotlight is aimed in the right direction, this kind of beauty and creativity can draw us into God's holy presence. But sometimes, the spotlight subtly shifts off of God and onto us.

For whatever reason, this particular night felt off. I couldn't shake the feeling that the moment was screaming, *Me! Me! Me! It's all about me!* After the fog cleared, the Anglican bishop stepped onto the stage, dressed in what I can only describe as bishop attire—the kind of outfit that says, "I've never used a fog machine." He walked up to the microphone and began with what sounded like a four-hundred-year-old prayer.

The contrast was jarring.

The words were ancient. Familiar. Weighty.

Now, those are words I could moor my life to, I thought.

While I couldn't tell you the exact selection from the Book of Common Prayer he read that night, I do know the words he spoke didn't flatter. They didn't present Jesus as a self-help guru promising your best life now. They conveyed something deeper: that following Jesus isn't about getting God on our terms, but reorienting our lives around him.

I had the immediate and overwhelming sense that I'd been sipping Coca-Cola—and N. T. Wright had just handed me a glass of aged wine.

I understand wanting to debunk the image of a distant, angry God. I want people to know that God loves them and they don't have to clean themselves up before drawing near. I want everybody to experience firsthand that God doesn't just love us, he actually likes us. But is it possible that, in our desire for intimacy, we sometimes forget the gravity of the one we're approaching?

We don't need a God who is like us. We need a God who's not like us.

A God who can draw us up out of our own small selves and into something far larger. We don't need a lighter faith; we need a weightier, more substantive summons to a life of otherness. We need a way of approaching God that does justice to who he truly is and then reshapes us in his image.

So what do we do? Where do we turn when God feels both near and wild, loving and untamable?

We pray, "Holy be your name," because these words invite us to reorient our lives around a presence that's real, radiant, and, honestly, a little risky.

WHAT HOLINESS REALLY MEANS

You may be more familiar with the King James Version of this line of Jesus' prayer: "Hallowed be thy name" (Matthew 6:9). To hallow something means "to treat it as holy" or "to revere it."[2] In Hebrew, the word translated as "holy"—*qudosh*—means "separate, unique, distinct, and set apart for a sacred purpose."[3]

Hallowed isn't a word we use much anymore, except for when we speak about hallowed ground. *Hallowed ground* refers to those places we treat as holy because something unique happened there. We all have places in our lives that hold that kind of significance.

What are the hallowed grounds in your life? Can you name what happened in those specific places to make them so sacred?

Maybe you grew up going to baseball games with your dad. Now, whenever you walk into a ballpark, you can't help but feel the depth of that connection. Perhaps your mom took you to an ice cream shop to celebrate your victories or to have meaningful conversations whenever you were down. Or think about the way certain historical locations affect us. Visitors who walk among the 9,387 white crosses at the Normandy American Cemetery in France don't speak in normal voices.[4] They whisper. Why? Because it's impossible to visit Normandy without being thunderstruck by the sense that this ground is different from other ground.

What makes these places holy is the fact that they're not like everything else.

Unfortunately, the word *holy* elicits all kinds of negative connotations. We think of people who are holier-than-thou or have an attitude of superiority. Holiness might sound cold and unattainable. It could bring to mind stuffy religious people who never have any fun because they're so busy pretending they're better than everybody else. And that's tragic, because biblical holiness is radiant.

I love the way BibleProject has explained it. Essentially their view is:

> God's holiness is like the sun. There's nothing like it in our solar system. It's utterly unique and extremely powerful. It's the life-giving source sustaining all that's good on our planet. In that sense, the sun is holy. Of course, if you get too close, that same power will destroy you.[5]

In the Bible, God's holiness functions in a similar way. In 2 Samuel 6, King David and thirty thousand of his closest friends traveled to Judah to bring the ark of God up to Jerusalem. To move it, they built a new cart and hitched it to a team of oxen. Along the way, David and his companions were celebrating with all their might when tragedy struck. One of the oxen stumbled, and a man named Uzzah—who was helping transport the ark—reached out and grabbed the ark to steady it. Suddenly, "The LORD's anger burned against Uzzah because of his irreverent act; therefore God struck him down, and he died there beside the ark of God" (v. 7).

Honestly, I don't like this story, and neither did King David. The text says, "David was angry . . . [and] afraid . . . and said, 'How can the ark of the LORD ever come to me?'" (2 Samuel 6:8–9).

It's almost like God was saying, "I'm not your mascot. You and your friends don't get to parade me around like a trophy or some prized possession. That's not how this works."

But as disturbing as that story is, we encounter dangerous goodness on a daily basis.

When I put my teenager behind the wheel of a car, I want her to understand it's not a toy. When used carelessly, its power can be lethal. Chainsaws are an amazing piece of technology. I don't have the science to back this up, but I'm pretty sure that just standing near one boosts testosterone. But it's a perilous power if not used with caution.

I get it. God isn't a chainsaw or a car. He's personal. He's relational. Which is exactly what makes stories like Uzzah's so jarring. When someone you love is distant, it's one kind of pain. When someone you love is dangerous—when their closeness carries risk—that's another thing altogether.

But God's holiness isn't dangerous because he's volatile or reckless or cruel. It's dangerous because we're fragile. His greatness and power don't diminish to fit our expectations. He comes as he is: pure, radiant, and blazing. And the gap between his purity and our presumption is what makes the ground shake.

C. S. Lewis captured this dynamic perfectly in *The Lion, the Witch, and the Wardrobe* when Mr. Beaver tells the Pevensie children about Aslan:

"Safe?" said Mr. Beaver. "Who said anything about safe? 'Course he isn't safe. But he's good. He's the King, I tell you."[6]

Which is why, in God's kindness, he puts certain boundaries in place, not to keep us away, but to keep us alive.

For instance, when Moses asked to see God's glory, God replied by saying, "'I will cause all my goodness to pass in front of you, and I will proclaim my name, the Lord, in your presence . . . But,' he said, 'you cannot see my face, for no one may see me and live'" (Exodus 33:19–20).

God didn't just spare Moses' life; he made a way for him to approach holiness and be transformed by it. And when Moses came down the mountain, his transformation was obvious—so obvious, the people were terrified. But Moses "was not aware that his face was radiant because he had spoken with the Lord" (Exodus 34:29).

When Jesus teaches us to pray, "Holy be your name," he's inviting us into something similar—a way of approaching God's holiness that holds fascination and reverence together and changes us in the process.

And if God's holiness is this radiant and powerful, the question becomes: How do we treat his name? How do we live in response to it?

Not casually or flippantly.

We treat it with awe. With reverence. With the kind of holy fear that doesn't push us away from God, but draws us closer, trembling with wonder.

FEARING AND REVERING

Had the tourists I mentioned earlier balanced their awe with a dose of healthy fear, they could've avoided harm, not to mention the horror of going viral. In Jesus' world, the fear of the LORD was a big deal. Proverbs famously says, "The fear of the LORD is the beginning of knowledge" (1:7). The book of Job is even more direct, saying simply, "The fear of the Lord—that is wisdom" (28:28).

But how is this fear supposed to work? Are we truly meant to be afraid of God?

Well, yes and no. This is where understanding the language makes a huge difference.

In Hebrew, the word for fear is *yir'ah*, and it has a range of meanings. In one sense, it means exactly what it sounds like: terror.[7]

Recently, I was snorkeling with my youngest daughter when, suddenly, a shark swam underneath us. Although our heads were underwater, I heard her scream echo through the ocean. In a flash, she was climbing up my back and trying to perch atop my head like a pelican on a buoy. Naturally, this drove my face deeper, sending water gushing down my snorkel.

The Scriptures are full of moments when people react the same way when they realize they're in the presence of the Holy One.[8] God starts many conversations in the Bible by saying, "Don't be afraid," for good reason.

So *yir'ah* means terror, but it also means awe or wonder—the mysterious feeling of amazement you get in the presence of something massive and powerful that we talked about a few chapters ago.

Then there's the dimension of *yir'ah* that means reverent respect.

Together, those definitions convey terror, awe, and reverent respect. Which one are we supposed to feel toward God?

All three, actually. This threefold idea of fear as terror, awe, and reverent respect was baked into the Israelite imagination, and it's why Jesus taught us to approach God in prayer with the words, "Holy be your name."

Take a kitchen stove, for example. Small children can't yet grasp its usefulness or power, so to keep them safe, we teach them to fear it: *Hot! Don't touch!* But as they grow, that fear matures into understanding. They come to see the stove not as something to be afraid of, but as something powerful—something good. It's not a threat. It's a tool. A gift, even, but one that demands respect. We don't want our kids to be afraid forever. We want them to grow by learning to relate to the power with a respect that helps them engage it wisely.

But what happens when the dangerous goodness you're approaching isn't a kitchen appliance, but the holy God of the universe? That's what Jesus is trying to drive home by teaching us to approach God in prayer with the words, "Holy be your name." It's not a formula—it's a posture of the heart.

In the Hebrew Bible, the way to approach God's holiness with reverence and respect was through purification. You'd avoid contact with anything associated with death: diseases, dead bodies, or certain bodily fluids. And that meant steering clear of anything or anyone that was impure, because impurity was essentially contagious. You'd set yourself apart so you wouldn't profane God's holy presence.

All this comes into sharp focus in an experience between God and the prophet Isaiah. At one point God gave the prophet a vision of the heavenly temple, and Isaiah described it like this: "I saw the Lord, high and exalted, seated on a throne" (Isaiah 6:1).

Sounds pretty awesome, right? Apparently not.

"Woe to me!" [Isaiah] cried. "I am ruined! For I am a man of unclean lips, and I live among a people of unclean lips" (v. 5).

In God's holy presence, Isaiah was terrified, not because it was bad, but because it was so good.[9] It was so pure, so illuminating, that it exposed how shabby he and his people truly were.

God didn't summon Isaiah because he needed an ego boost or to soak him in a shame shower—*look how awful you are!* God summoned Isaiah because he was looking for a partner.

But how do you partner with a holy God when you're a broken, sinful person?

You rely on God to make a way.

God did for Isaiah what Isaiah never could have done for himself: A heavenly being touched Isaiah's lips with a hot coal from the heavenly altar and declared, "Your guilt is taken away and your sin atoned for" (v. 7).

Isaiah suddenly realized that in God's presence, holiness—not impurity—was contagious.

This is a vision that anticipates something Jesus would perfectly embody. Instead of being defiled by lepers, the sick, and the demon possessed, Jesus' touch would purify them!

After the coal, in verse 8, God got to the point of Isaiah's vision and asked, "Whom shall I send? And who will go for us?"

And Isaiah answered, "Here am I. Send me!"

Do you see what happened? First, Isaiah was terrified. Then, he understood, and that gave him the courage to step forward as God's partner. What began in terror grew into understanding and matured into a reverent and respectful collaboration.

Isaiah's experience was a taste of what God had always intended for his people, and what he intends for us still. Praying, "Holy be your name" is stepping toward the blazing center of God's holiness—not to be crushed by it, but to be changed by it—so we can carry his presence into the world.

HOLINESS AT THE CENTER

During the Israelites' formative wilderness journey, God told Moses, "Have them [the Israelites] make a sanctuary for me, and I will dwell among them" (Exodus 25:8). God wasn't looking for a building. He was making a way to be present with his people. His desire wasn't simply proximity, but participation. He wanted to dwell with them at the center of their shared life.

The Israelites understood that God is so vast, he fills the heavens—yet he is also powerful enough to localize his presence in a specific place. And that place was the sanctuary (tabernacle).

But how could a holy God dwell among an unholy people? The layout of the camp offered a visual answer. In Numbers 2, God instructed the Israelites to camp in formation—three tribes on each side of the tabernacle, positioned at a distance, with God's dwelling at the center (v. 2).

The design was a daily reminder: God is the blazing center, and everything else is meant to orbit around him. His presence isn't something we approach casually; it's something we stand in awe of. And it's something we're invited to center our lives around.

That invitation still holds. When God is at the center, everything—our time, our relationships, our money—takes its shape around him. But if we're honest, we often do the opposite. We place ourselves at the center and push God to the margins, hoping he'll conform to our wants, our needs, our plans.

Want to know what's at the center of your life? Watch where your time, money, and attention go. Your calendar, your receipts, your screen time—they're all telling a story about what you revere. Push God's transforming presence to the periphery, and you won't just lose sight of him; you'll inevitably recast him in your own image.

I don't know how that lands with you, but I know me.

While I do believe God intends us to become the best version of ourselves, the only way that happens is by becoming like him. As C. S. Lewis said, "God became man to turn creatures into sons and daughters: not simply to produce better men or women of the old kind but to produce a new kind of human."[10]

He came to make us into himself.

When God takes center stage, things start falling into their rightful place. Peace returns. Priorities shift. We stop living for our own small kingdoms and start longing for his.

A FAITHFUL ACHE

Make no mistake, though; putting God at the center won't make your life easier. Start reflecting a God who's set apart, and you won't blend in so easily with a world that bows to other gods—comfort, control, success, safety, and the self. You'll stand out. You'll feel the friction of living according to a different center of gravity. But guess what? You may not actually mind because you'll start to feel a faithful ache.

In a consumer culture, one of the strangest things about Christians is their commitment to give away a portion of their income. It's a way of acknowledging that God is generous, and that he's entrusted us with his resources. As we're transformed by him, we start to reflect his generosity by becoming generous ourselves.

Several years ago, my wife and I kept noticing the money in our bank account was stressfully low. This continued for months, until—one day—things boiled over.

"Is someone stealing from us?" I asked.

"I know," she said. "I don't understand what's happening. We're being so careful."

So we went through our transaction history with a fine-tooth comb and discovered the money wasn't "disappearing" to Chipotle; we were actually "giving" more than we realized. Now, lest you assume I've included this story as a humble-brag, believe me when I say: It wasn't a lot of money. But at that time in our lives, it was a lot of money for us!

Knowing the money was being given didn't change the situation. We still had cash-flow problems, but it dramatically changed how we felt about it. It turned into a faithful ache.

We feel the faithful ache when we take care of our bodies by getting active and working out, but unlike the ache your body feels when neglected, this is the delicious ache in your muscles that says, *I showed up.*

Or think about people like Martin Luther King Jr. and Rosa Parks being arrested for their work in the civil rights movement. I assume there's nothing easy about being thrown in jail, but when it's for the right reason, you undoubtedly feel different about it. It becomes a badge of honor—a faithful ache.

So be warned: When you place God's holy name at the center of your life, and it starts wearing off on you, it will create tension. But it's a tension you'll welcome—a holy tension that reshapes you from the inside out.

Praying "Holy be your name" is how we stay centered and recalibrated for this new way of being in the world. Because we don't become our truest selves until our lives orbit the blazing center of his presence.

WHAT'S SITTING AT YOUR CENTER?

Every one of us already has something sitting at the center of our lives, a touchpoint we orbit around. Maybe in your house it's the fridge. If you're on the road a lot, maybe it's the dashboard in your vehicle. Or, if you're like me, it's your phone.

In *Gulliver's Travels,* when the people of Lilliput searched Gulliver and found his watch, they assumed it was his god—because he never did anything without consulting it first.[11]

I can relate. My phone goes everywhere I do. It holds my calendar, my photos, my messages and calls. I hate that it's true, but it's usually the first thing I touch in the morning, and the last thing I touch before switching off the light at night. So here's a simple invitation: Choose something that sits at the center of your life, some physical object your life naturally orbits around—your phone, your fridge, your computer—and put the words "Holy be your name" on that thing. If it's your phone or your computer, make those words your background. If it's your fridge, put up a Post-it note.

Let it be a visual disruptor, something to nudge you back to the truth that God—not self—is meant to sit at the center. Because when he's there, everything else finds its rightful place—and his holiness radiates through us into the world.

CHAPTER 7

MAKE US YOUR REPRESENTATIVES

Holy Be Your Name

BRAD GRAY

There's a beloved Jewish tale about Rabbi Akiva walking home from the synagogue one evening.[1] Like many rabbis, Akiva used his commute to meditate on the Scriptures. Deeply engrossed in his recitation, he failed to notice a fork in the road and took the wrong path.

Suddenly, a voice thundered out of the darkness above, saying, "Who are you? What are you doing here?"

Startled, Akiva realized his mistake. Instead of walking home, he'd wandered to a Roman military outpost!

Again, the voice roared, "Who are you? What are you doing here?"

Regaining his composure, Akiva answered the question with a question: "How much do you get paid a day?"

Thrown off, the soldier answered, "I get paid two denarii a day, Jew. Why?"

"Because I'll double your wage," said Akiva, "if you stand outside the gate of my house and ask me those two questions every morning."

Who are you?

What are you doing here?

We ask these questions with special urgency early in life, but they never really go away. I regularly meet people in their forties, fifties, and sixties still trying to answer them. Life keeps changing, and so do we. Different seasons ask different things of us. But through it all, we long to live with purpose. To know that our lives mean something.

People in the Bible had that same desire for identity and direction. When Jesus taught his disciples to pray, "Holy be your name," he wasn't just reminding them to revere God's name; he was calling them to represent it. He was pointing to an identity and mission that stretched all the way back to the exodus.

In this chapter, we'll explore what it means that God rescued his people not only *from* something but *for* something. Their calling wasn't generic. It was bound up with his name, something they needed to be reminded of every day.

We're no different. Our world is filled with noise—a cacophony of voices all too ready to define who we are and why we're here.

You are what you achieve (success).
You are what you produce (hustle).
You are what you own (consumerism).
You are how you measure up (social media).
You are what was done to you (wounds and trauma).
You are the group you belong to (partisan identity).
You are what you've done (shame).

These voices are persistent and often persuasive. But none of them holds a candle to the person God is calling you to be or the story he's inviting you to live. Praying, "Holy be your name" helps you recover your true identity and learn to carry his name well in a world that's desperate to know what he's like.

A NAME AND A PEOPLE

Here's a pattern in Scripture I wonder if you've noticed: Before God tells people how to live, he begins by telling them who they are.

One of the most obvious examples is found in the book of Ephesians. For the first three chapters, Paul didn't give his readers a single command. Instead, he told them who they were: *You're chosen, you're adopted, you're God's handiwork*. It was only after establishing their identity in Christ that he started talking about behavior. Why?

Because behavior flows from identity. Knowing who you are clarifies what you should do.

Something similar happens in the book of Exodus. Right before giving the Israelites the Ten Commandments, God gave them something else: a new identity. He said, "If you obey me fully and keep my covenant, then out of all nations you will be my treasured possession. Although the whole earth is mine, you will be for me a kingdom of priests and a holy nation" (Exodus 19:5–6).

The force of this passage is conveyed in three distinct phrases: "treasured possession," "kingdom of priests," and "holy nation."

"Treasured possession" comes from the Hebrew word *segullah,* which is a technical term used in treaty contexts to designate someone as the king's authorized representative.[2] Being a representative is serious business. Our expression, "Don't shoot me, I'm just the messenger" conveys a certain distance. It says, *I don't have a dog in this fight. I'm separate from the message.* Representatives, on the other hand, speak *for* and *as* the one they represent. What's more, *segullah* implies deep relational closeness. God was offering the Israelites a new identity by entering into an intimate relationship with them.

"Kingdom of priests" would have had special resonance for the Israelites since they had just left Egypt. More gods and goddesses have been identified in ancient Egypt than any other society in human history, and each had their own priests serving as mediators. The priests represented the people to the gods and the gods to the people. Old Testament scholar Dr. Carmen Imes put it well: "The Israelites lived in a time when people were desperate to know what the gods were saying."[3] And priests had the one thing everyone was most desperate for: access to the divine.

"Holy nation" is what set Israel apart. Egyptian priests managed the divine, but they weren't expected to become like the gods they served. Israel, by contrast, was called to *embody* the holiness of the God they represented. Holiness wasn't just something they handled; it was something they were meant to mirror.

This kind of identity—being chosen to reflect God's holiness—isn't simply an ancient story or abstract theology; it's meant to show up in our daily lives today.

Brad Nelson, my coauthor, has a friend named Herb who's an ordained priest. He rides a Harley and smokes a pipe, and, as you might expect, his path to the priesthood was somewhat unusual.

It started when he became a hospice chaplain. Herb was in and out of the hospital constantly. He'd show up dressed in his street clothes and get harassed by the hospital staff wanting to know who he was and what he was doing there. It was constant. Eventually, he got so fed up with it, he bought a priestly collar. Before walking into the hospital, he'd put on the collar, and, just like that, people stopped interrogating him. They saw the collar and did the math.

But the collar didn't just stop the questions. It prompted new ones. Strangers would ask him, "Father, could you bless me?" Or, "Father, will you pray for my mom? She's sick." Everywhere he went, his clothing seemed to announce, *Here is someone with access to God.* People would see him and think, *I'm not capable of talking to God myself, but that guy can help!*

These encounters were so moving and so frequent, he decided to make it official and seek ordination.

By wearing the collar, Herb got a taste of what it means to be God's priestly representative. It's a remarkable shift when you think about it—from ordinary guy to God's ambassador. It must have felt that way for the Israelites too—going from voiceless slaves to priests who represented the God of the universe.

And God intended to make the most of it.

He strategically dropped them at the crossroads of the ancient world. Biblical geographers refer to Canaan as a "land between"[4] because it sat at the nexus of three continents: Africa, Asia, and Europe. It linked the great empires of Egypt and Mesopotamia, bridged the Red Sea and the Mediterranean Sea, and served as a hub for trade, travel, and cultural exchange.

It's as if God said, "I want you *here*, where the world passes through. Be my living message—my hands and feet—so when people encounter you, it'll be as if they're encountering me."

How the Israelites conducted business, treated vulnerable people, and practiced justice and righteousness was supposed to stand out. They were meant to provoke curiosity, so others would wonder, *Who are these people? Why do they live this way? Who is their God?*

The same is meant to be true for us.

When we stand at the crossroads of culture, though, the real question becomes: *Who's shaping whom*?

To keep his people distinct, God gave them visual reminders—daily, tactile cues to help them remember who they were and what they were there for.

FREEDOM IN RESTRAINT

In Numbers 15, God gave the Israelites this peculiar instruction: "Make tassels on the corners of your garments, with a blue cord on each tassel. You will have these tassels to look at and so you will remember all the commands of the LORD" (vv. 38–39).

This passage from Numbers is actually part of the Shema—the ancient practice of reciting sections of Scripture from Deuteronomy 6, Deuteronomy 11, and Numbers 15 every morning and every evening. A religious Jew will recite these words over twenty thousand times in their lifetime. The daily reciting of the Shema would've been part of Jesus' daily rhythms as well.

According to Numbers 15, the tassels represented God's commandments. Sometimes the word *commandments* can sound rigid, impersonal, like, "Do this or else." We tend to think of God's law as something burdensome, but that's not how the Torah was viewed in the ancient Jewish world.

We often translate *Torah* as "law," but that's a bit misleading. Hebrew is a verb-based language, and the noun *Torah* comes from the verb *yarah*, which means "to teach" or "to instruct."[5] Another word derived from *yarah* is *moreh*, which means "teacher." So Torah literally means "teachings" or "instructions." These are God's instructions for life—dynamic, personal, and relational. They're not cold legal codes. They're meant to help God's people flourish.

Remember how God rescued his people not only from something but for something? We see the same thing in the Torah. It's a concept David Brooks articulated beautifully when he wrote, "In our culture we think of freedom as the absence of restraint. That's *freedom from*. But there is another, higher kind of freedom. That is *freedom to*. This is the freedom as fullness of capacity, and it often involves restriction and restraint."[6]

Jazz musicians are a case in point. They have a seemingly limitless capacity, but that freedom is the result of years and years of discipline, practice, and restraint. It's the same with the Torah.

Psalm 119 gives us a beautiful picture of this: "I run in the path of your commands, for you have set my heart *free*. . . . Direct me in the path of your commands, for there I find *delight*. . . . I will walk about in *freedom*, for I have sought out your precepts" (vv. 32, 35, 45, emphasis added).

God's commandments aren't about control; they're about freedom. They show us how to thrive in the world he made.

Think about ways this is true today. The freedom of a flourishing marriage is a direct result of the restraint of fidelity. The freedom of operating as a trusted business is a direct result of the restraint of honesty and integrity. The freedom of not having financial troubles is a direct result of the restraint of living within a budget.

What restrictions and restraints have unleashed a deeper level of freedom in your life?

A ROYAL REMINDER

The tassels reminded the Israelites that God's instructions for life would help them flourish—and it brought to mind the new identity he had given them.

So every glance at the corner of an Israelite's garment would whisper: *I belong to God. His ways are good. Be faithful.*

A striking detail in Numbers 15 is God's instruction for each tassel to include a blue cord. In the ancient world, blue was extremely rare. It could only be extracted from the *Murex trunculus* snail, found along the Mediterranean coasts of northern Israel and Lebanon. Baruch Sterman, cofounder of the Ptil Tekhelet center in Jerusalem and a leading expert on biblical blue, estimates that it took one hundred snails to dye just four threads blue![7] Because of its scarcity and cost, blue was reserved for people of high standing or royalty—hence the term *royal blue*.

The blue cord pointed to the Israelites' value as God's treasured possession. What a powerful daily reminder.

But there's even more going on.

According to Exodus 28:31, the robe of the high priest was to be made entirely of blue, making it the most prominent color of his sacred garments. In addition, he was to wear a white turban with a gold plate affixed to the front, engraved with the words *kadosh la-YHWH*—"Holy to the Lord" (Exodus 28:36). It was a bold declaration—worn across his forehead, carried into the presence of God, and seen by the people.

And how was that gold plate fastened to his turban?

With "a blue cord" (v. 37)—the same "blue cord" God instructed to be woven into every Israelite tassel.

The high priest bore God's name publicly, visibly, and unmistakably. And in a way, so did everyone else. Like a jersey stitched with a last name across the back, the tassels were a kind of uniform—a visible reminder that they weren't just individuals. They were a kingdom of priests, bearing God's name, with a royal calling to represent him well in the world.

We all need reminders. In a world constantly trying to define us, label us, box us in, and tell us who we're supposed to be, we need something to pull us back to the truth of who we are. That's why, when I'm dropping my kids off at school or sports practice, I'll often remind them, "Remember, your last name is Gray. You're not just representing yourself—you're representing our family. And more importantly, you represent Jesus. So represent us well."

Saying yes to Jesus means we've been invited into a bigger story—the story of a people chosen, holy, and royal. Not for our own privilege, but for his purpose. A people marked to make his name known. To live lives that say, "Holy be your name."

CARRYING THE NAME

As we've already seen, names in the ancient world weren't just labels. They revealed a person's character, identity, and mission. God's name is a big deal. Which is why out of the Ten Commandments, only one carried the threat of severe punishment, and it's not the one you'd expect.

Murder? Nope.

Adultery? Think again.

It's the command about God's name: "You shall not take the name of the Lord your God in vain, for the Lord will not hold him guiltless who takes his name in vain" (Exodus 20:7 ESV).

People have wrestled with the meaning of this command for centuries. Dr. Imes identified twenty-three different ways it's been interpreted throughout history![8] Some say it forbids false oaths, like swearing to tell the truth in God's name and then lying. Others say it's about cursing. That's the one that was hammered into my head as a kid.

But the Hebrew language reveals something far deeper—and more serious.

The word translated "to take" is *nasa*, meaning "to lift up, to bear, or to carry."[9] The word for "vain" is *shav*, meaning "vanity, nothingness, or emptiness."[10] In essence, God was saying, "Don't carry my name as though it's nothing." Picture the Israelites physically carrying God's name with them, like a badge of identity and belonging.

This language appears again on the heels of the priestly blessing in Numbers 6, the blessing that Aaron, the high priest, and his sons spoke over the Israelites: "The Lord bless you and keep you; the Lord make his face shine upon you and be gracious to you; the Lord turn his face toward you and give you peace" (vv. 24–26). It's a powerful blessing.

Equally as powerful is what God said in the very next verse: "They will put my name on the Israelites, and I will bless them" (v. 27). With this blessing, God put his name on the people. Aaron, the high priest, bore God's holy name, and so did the Israelites.

The Psalms are full of links between God's name and his people's behavior, such as Psalm 45:17: "I will cause your name to be celebrated in all generations; therefore the peoples will praise you forever and ever" (NRSV).

This idea of building respect for God's name through one's behavior is called *sanctifying the name* in Judaism. Rabbi Jonathan Sacks explained that it "is no mere marginal addendum to the script of Jewish life but its very point: to bring God's presence into the world by making others aware that God's word sanctifies life."[11]

As a first-century Jewish teacher, Jesus' life was deeply rooted in the idea of "sanctifying the name." As we've already seen, the Lord's Prayer bears a striking resemblance to another well-known Jewish prayer dating to the time of Jesus, the *Kaddish*. Its opening words? "Magnified and sanctified be Your great name."[12]

In the words of J. H. Hertz, "The Jew should remember that the glory of God is, as it were, entrusted to his care, and that every Israelite holds the honor of his faith and of his entire people in his hands."[13]

No pressure, then.

PROFANING THE NAME

The idea that God's glory has been entrusted to our care is a sobering thought—one that hit home for me on a recent family vacation in Cancún. One day while my kids were playing at the beach, I had an unexpected encounter with God's name at a tiki hut.

Seated on a swing at the tiki hut was a woman who'd clearly had too much to drink. Wearing a skimpy bathing suit, she was belting out a song and slurring her words in a way that drew everyone's attention.

Drunken tourists aren't unusual in Cancún. What *was* unusual was her tattoo. Prominently situated on her arm for all the world to see was God's personal four-letter name: *YHWH.*

I carried our drinks back to the beach with a pit in my stomach. It was the same feeling I get when I hear yet another story of a Christian leader's public failure. When we don't carry God's name well, we misrepresent him to the watching world. When we blow it, it's not just our name we drag through the mud, it's his.

But that moment at the tiki hut was a gut check for another reason. It got me thinking about all the quiet, ordinary ways I do the same. Because carrying God's name isn't just about what's tattooed on our skin or stitched on our shirts. It's about how we live. How we speak. How we treat people, and the choices we make when no one's watching.

We bear the name, but with great privilege comes great responsibility. And like us, Israel struggled. Big time.

Instead of being a compelling counterculture—instead of giving the world a beautiful picture of the life God's holy name made possible—Israel forgot their identity and behaved like everyone else.

The prophet Amos named their profanity with searing clarity: "They sell the righteous for silver, and the needy for a pair of sandals—those who trample the head of the poor into the dust of the earth and turn aside the way of the afflicted; a man and his father go in to the same girl, so that my holy name is profaned" (Amos 2:6–7 ESV).

So God sent his people into exile.

But this created a new problem.

With the people in exile, God's reputation took a hit among the nations. You can practically hear the Babylonian taunts: "If your God is so great, where is he now?"

And God, who is always mindful of the way his name is used, took notice. Speaking through the prophet Ezekiel, God said, "It is not for your sake, people of Israel, that I am going to do these things, but for the sake of my holy name, which you have profaned among the nations where you have gone. I will show the holiness of my great name . . . Then the nations will know that I am the Lord . . . when I am proved holy through you before their eyes" (Ezekiel 36:22–23).

Centuries later, God did intervene. And this time, he showed them exactly what it looked like to carry the name well.

How did he do it? Jesus of Nazareth.

Scripture describes Jesus as "the radiance of God's glory and the exact representation of his being" (Hebrews 1:3). He is the Word of God in human form, and "the Word became flesh and made his dwelling among us" (John 1:14). That word *dwelling* means "tabernacle." Just like the tabernacle in the wilderness, Jesus was God's radiant presence that had come to dwell at the center of people's lives—demonstrating how to become a holy people who bear the name well and live from their God-given identity.

"Holy be your name" encompasses all of that, and Jesus invites us to pray these words daily as a ritual of remembrance.

Like Akiva, we need daily reminders about who we are and what we're doing here, because life has a way of calling into question that which is deepest in us. We get misnamed, labeled in ways that undermine the good gift God put us here to be and to give on his behalf. Names like *failure, hopeless, sensitive, overlooked, the pretty one, too much*, and *not enough*. "Holy be your name" is our daily guide back to the truth:

I belong to God. He determines who I am—chosen, holy, royal—and he has brought me into his bigger story.

I follow his ways, which honors him and frees me to flourish.

I'm wearing his name. I'm set apart so the world can see him through me—it's my great privilege and his sacred purpose.

WALKING THE TALK OF JESUS

When God acts in history, he does so through people. One of the first things Jesus did after launching his ministry was to gather a community of disciples—people who would emulate his way of life, not just his words.

The apostle Peter, writing to both Jewish and Gentile followers of Jesus in Asia Minor, reminded them of who they were: "You are a chosen people, a royal priesthood, a holy nation, God's special possession, that you may declare the praises of him who called you out of darkness into his wonderful light. . . . Live such good lives among the pagans that, though they accuse you of doing wrong, they may see your good deeds and glorify God" (1 Peter 2:9, 12).

Take these words to heart as someone who has given allegiance to King Jesus, and remember that every choice you make, every way you show up in the world, is telling a story about the God you belong to.

The only questions are: What message is your life communicating? and, Is it the message you want to be sending?

You don't have to be perfect. The first disciples weren't. But they kept walking with Jesus, learning, adjusting, and letting their lives slowly be shaped by the holiness of his name.

So can you.

When you pray, "Holy be your name," you're not just revering God—you're asking him to reshape your life into a living reflection of his.

You're inviting him to make his name great through you.

So ask: *Lord, shape me.*

Help me carry your name well.

And cause the world to see who you truly are.

CHAPTER 8

BRING YOUR GOOD RULE THROUGH US

Your Kingdom Come

BRAD GRAY

Americans are obsessed with royalty. In 1997, approximately 2.5 billion people tuned in to watch Princess Diana's funeral—nearly half of the world's population at the time![1] Between 2016 and 2020, Netflix estimates more than 73 million households streamed its hit series *The Crown*.[2] We can't seem to get enough of kings and queens.

And we're not alone. Across cultures, myths tell of a once-great king who ruled with justice and humility. Under his reign, people flourished. Then, in these myths, something always happens—the king goes away, and the kingdom falls into corruption and ruin. But the people never forget. They long for the day when the true king will return.

In the early 1990s, pastor Tim Keller asked, "Despite humanity's abysmal record of kingship, why is it that so many cultures preserve the same basic story?"

His answer?

"The reason we adore kings is because there is a memory trace in the human race . . . of a great King, an ancient King . . . we know we were built to submit to that King, to stand before and adore and serve and know that King."[3]

Maybe that's why, even today, we feel the restless ache that things aren't the way they're supposed to be.

That ache echoes in us as we read headlines: school shootings, broken institutions, people in poverty without access to clean water, the enduring presence of racism, the endless wars.

It reverberates closer to home too—in the broken relationships that accumulate over the course of a lifetime. In family gatherings that resurrect old wounds. In the loneliness and social disconnection that hang over our hyperconnected world like an invisible blanket. Not to mention all the ways our relentless striving—after success, perfection, and control—keep letting us down. It's as if our strategies for securing the good life keep backfiring.

What about you? Where do you feel that ache most viscerally?

Like every generation before us, we're waiting.

Waiting for a King who can set things right.

Waiting for justice to roll down like waters.

Waiting for peace to push back the chaos.

Waiting for wholeness to mend what's been shattered.

But what if the waiting is only half the story?

What if the King has already come and we're not just waiting for him, but being invited to join him—summoned to carry his kingdom into the cracks and crevices of a broken world?

The Lord's Prayer isn't simply a collection of comforting words for people longing for change. It announces a revolution. In order to understand who Jesus is and what he came to do, we have to focus on the very center of his message.

THE MOST EXPLOSIVE AND IMPORTANT PART

The structure of the Sermon on the Mount isn't random. It's layered and intentional—shaped with care to highlight what matters most. Like the other Gospel writers, Matthew faithfully preserves Jesus' teaching while also arranging it in a way that deliberately draws our attention to the center, where he wants us to hear his loudest shout: *Look here! This is the heart and soul of it all!*

If we had to summarize Jesus' teaching in a single word, it would be *kingdom.* Jesus explained the kingdom in his teachings, illustrated it in his parables, and embodied it in his signs, wonders, and shared meals. It's what he talked about more than anything else. In fact, the word *kingdom* appears more than fifty times in Matthew's gospel alone.

In Western culture, we tend to save the best for last—the grand finale at a fireworks show or the final scene of a movie. But the Bible often does the opposite, placing the most important material at the center like a literary sandwich.

And that's exactly what Matthew does with the Sermon on the Mount.

The sermon itself is arranged into three broad sections:[4]

Introduction (Matthew 5:3–16)
Body (Matthew 5:17–7:12)
Conclusion (Matthew 7:13–27)

Zoom in closer, and you'll see that the body—the central section—also divides into three parts:

Righteousness toward the Torah (Matthew 5:17–48)
Righteousness toward God (Matthew 6:1–18)
Righteousness in everyday living (Matthew 6:19–7:12)

Zoom in even closer, and the section on *righteousness toward God* divides again into three practices:

Almsgiving (Matthew 6:1–4)
Prayer (Matthew 6:5–15)
Fasting (Matthew 6:16–18)[5]

And right at the center of the center of the center—what do we find? The Lord's Prayer. Matthew is doing everything in his written power to shout: "Look here! This is the heart and soul of it all!"

Zoom in one final time, and at the very center of the Lord's Prayer itself we find the heartbeat of it all: "Your kingdom come, your will be done, on earth as it is in heaven" (Matthew 6:10).

These lines are the most explosive and important part of the entire prayer. The kingdom of heaven is ground zero in the Jesus story. In fact, it's the core idea of the Bible, and it runs from Genesis all the way to Revelation. It's here, in the Lord's Prayer, where Jesus articulates how this idea is meant to transform our lives and bring rescue and healing to the world.

If we fail to grasp what Jesus means by kingdom, not only will we misunderstand who he is and why he came, but we'll misconstrue what it means to follow him.

Words matter—these words especially. Our words shape our world and have a way of becoming flesh. As we've said before, Jesus didn't leave us the Lord's Prayer so we could merely recite words. He gave it to us because when we place these words at the center of our life and they start to become flesh, it's like joining a revolution.

It shook people then.

It should still shake us now.

The problem is, it usually doesn't.

Somewhere along the way, we've softened it. Smoothed it out. Made it safe.

If we're going to hear Jesus the way his original audience did, we've got to recover what he actually meant by "kingdom." Once we do, it won't just unlock the beauty and power of the Bible—it'll reframe how we see the whole world, and ultimately, how we live within it.

Because this is the apex of the prayer—the turning point of the book—we're going to slow down and pull it apart piece by piece. Think of this chapter as the deep dive, so in the next one we can surface with fresh clarity about what this means for your actual, everyday life.

THE MAIN THEME OF THE BIBLE

When Jesus said, "kingdom," his audience didn't scratch their heads in confusion. They knew exactly what he meant. Kingdom is one of the Bible's main themes, running from Genesis to Revelation.

Genesis opens with, "In the beginning God created the heavens and the earth" (Genesis 1:1). Two realms. Two dimensions. Heaven is God's space, where his will is done. Earth is human space, entrusted to us.

In the beginning, they overlapped, and the whole thing pulsated with *shalom*—meaning not just peace, but wholeness and flourishing. Everything was in its proper place. This shalom held together four key relationships: God with people; people with each other; people with themselves; and people with the earth.

But shalom came with responsibility—which we can see in the way God created and commissioned humans.

In Genesis 1:26, God said, "Let us make mankind in our image." In the ancient Near East, only kings were said to bear the divine image. They even had statues (*tzelem* in Hebrew[6]) placed throughout their kingdoms as a visible reminder: *This is what the king is like.*[7] So when God said that *all humans* would bear his image, it's royal language and it's radical. We aren't making images of God. *We* are the image. Every person—man, woman, child—is a walking, talking reminder of what God is like.

Next, God appointed these image-bearers to "rule" and "subdue" the earth. Those words can feel heavy-handed to modern ears, like we're setting out for domination. But Genesis 2 clarifies what that rule looks like: "The LORD God took the man and put him in the Garden of Eden to *work it* and *take care of it*" (Genesis 2:15, emphasis added).

The Hebrew verb for "work" is *avad*, which means "to serve or worship."[8] The word for "take care of" is *shamar*, which means "to keep, to guard, to preserve, to nurture, or even to husband."[9] What's even more remarkable is that these two words show up later in the Bible to describe the work priests do.[10]

In other words, ruling and subduing aren't about domination. They're about delegation. This is royal stewardship. A priestly partnership.

Humans were created to show the nature of God and commissioned to co-rule with him as kings and queens, offering their work as a form of worship and service to nurture, preserve, and husband the world into flourishing. No wonder we're fascinated by royalty—it's an echo of our true calling.

But, as Eugene Peterson put it, "The taste for God is debased into a greed to be God."[11] Rather than ruling *with* God, humanity tried to rule without him. The result? Sin, death, pain, brokenness, chaos, and the separation of heaven and earth. The loss of shalom. Humans out of touch with the kingdom life they were meant for.

But God didn't give up on his people. He responded by choosing a man, Abraham, and promising, "I will make you into a great nation . . . you will be a blessing . . . all peoples on earth will be blessed through you" (Genesis 12:2–3).

Then Abraham's family ended up enslaved in Egypt. Again, God pursued, rescuing the people from Pharaoh's army through the parted waters of the Sea. When they realized they were free, the people sang, "The Lord reigns for ever and ever" (Exodus 15:18).

Welcome to the Bible's first explicit mention of God as king.

God was the Israelites' king, and at Mount Sinai, he gave them a new identity: "You will be for me a kingdom of priests and a holy nation" (Exodus 19:6). Once again, God called his people to live as royal, priestly representatives. They even built a tabernacle (which later became a temple) where heaven and earth would begin to overlap once again.

But old habits die hard. In 1 Samuel, the people told the prophet, "Appoint a king to lead us, such as all the other nations have" (8:5).

When Samuel became livid in response, God assured him, "It is not you they have rejected, but they have rejected me as their king" (v. 7).

God gave them what they asked for. The name of Israel's first king, fittingly, was *Shaul* (Saul), which means *asked for.* But—surprise!—Mr. Asked-For didn't do what the people asked for, and the kings, for the most part, turned out to be a disaster overall.

So God sent prophets—truth-tellers to call his people back. Many were ignored. Some were killed. Even as the prophets gave rebukes, they offered hope by speaking of a coming king: "A child is born . . . a son is given, and the government will be on his shoulders. . . . Of the greatness of his government and peace there will be no end. He will reign on David's throne and over his kingdom, establishing and upholding it with justice and righteousness from that time on and forever" (Isaiah 9:6–7).

Government. Peace. Reign. Throne. Kingdom.

God went on to fulfill these promises in a way no one could have fathomed—by becoming one of his people, revealing his presence in the flesh, and tabernacling among them.

THE REVOLUTION BEGINS

The stretch between the prophets' promises and Jesus' arrival spanned hundreds of years, so by the first century, the ache for the coming king had reached a fever pitch. Between the crushing taxes imposed by their Roman oppressors, the brutality of the Herodian puppet regime, and the disillusionment with their own religious leaders, the Jewish people were living in a powder keg. All they needed was a spark.

Enter John the Baptist: the wild-eyed, camel-hair-clad, desert-dwelling prophet with an electrifying message: "Repent, for the kingdom of heaven is near" (Matthew 3:2).

There it is—the kingdom again. And "is near" didn't mean it was getting close; it meant *now.* It was already breaking in.[12]

John wasn't what you would call "seeker-sensitive." He had a way of naming the truth that was both refreshing and disruptive. He told people that if they wanted change, the place to start was painfully obvious: themselves.

And people came in droves. They left the cities and wandered into the wilderness to confess their sins and be baptized.

John's message hit a nerve—especially with the powerful. He called the Pharisees and Sadducees a "brood of vipers" (not a term of endearment) and publicly denounced Herod Antipas for his scandalous relationship with his brother's wife (Matthew 3:7; Mark 6:18–19). John's following grew so large that some feared it could turn into a political movement.

It was during this time that Jesus went out to see John, and when John saw Jesus, he lit up: "Look, the Lamb of God, who takes away the sin of the world! This is the one I meant when I said, 'A man who comes after me has surpassed me' . . . the reason I came baptizing with water was that he might be revealed to Israel" (John 1:29–31).

Then something unexpected happened: Jesus asked to be baptized. Stunned, John tried to talk Jesus out of it. I imagine him pulling Jesus aside, knee-deep in the Jordan River, and whispering through gritted teeth, "What are you doing? I've been telling everyone you're the one person who *doesn't need* this. I think it sends mixed signals."

But Jesus responded, "Let it be so now; it is proper for us to do this to fulfill all righteousness" (Matthew 3:15).

And just like that, John relented.

Why? What did John suddenly understand?

It has to do with the kingdom.

It has to do with God creating the world with shalom, with the introduction of sin and subsequent separation of heaven and earth, and with the chaos that ensued without shalom. Jesus' words "fulfill all righteousness" were code for the moment when God would step into human history in an unprecedented way—not just to forgive sin, but to repair the whole thing.

Remember, when God created the world, shalom preserved the four core relationships: with God, others, self, and creation. Since sin fractured all four, "righteousness" became tied to putting things back into right relationships.

Growing up, I was taught righteousness meant right behavior. But in the Bible, it's so much more. It means the standard of right relationships—being rightly aligned both vertically and horizontally. With God. With others. With ourselves. With the world.

So what is the kingdom of God? It's the rule and reign of God advancing here on earth, bringing healing and wholeness by pushing out the chaos.

And Jesus was lighting a match to spark God's revolution as he stood next to John.

Did John get a flash of this in Jesus' eyes? Maybe. Even if he didn't, it would become undeniably evident when Jesus came up out of the water.

WHEN PEACE MEETS CHAOS

Matthew plainly explains the following jaw-dropping events like this: "At that moment heaven was opened, and he saw the Spirit of God descending like a dove and lighting on him. And a voice from heaven said, 'This is my Son, whom I love; with him I am well pleased'" (Matthew 3:16–17).

God spoke, and the Spirit of God hovered over the waters in the form of a dove.

Does that sound at all familiar to you?

We're back to the Principle of First Use. Where else does this imagery show up in our Scriptures, and what might that tell us about what Jesus is doing?

The first *explicit* reference to a dove appears in the story of Noah. After the great flood, Noah sent out a dove. When it didn't return, he knew the floodwaters had receded and the dove had found a place to land (Genesis 8). This signified that a new era in human history had begun.

The first *implicit* reference to a dove, however, occurs even earlier: "In the beginning, God created the heavens and the earth. Now the earth was formless and empty, darkness was over the surface of the deep, and the Spirit of God was hovering over the waters. And God said, 'Let there be light,' and there was light" (Genesis 1:1–3).

The Hebrew root word for "hovering" is *rachaph*, which means "to flutter," as in "a bird flutters."[13] If you're thinking "dove" here, you're not the only one—a Jewish work called the Babylonian Talmud likened the hovering of God's spirit here in Genesis 1 to the hovering of a dove![14]

At creation, God spoke, and the Spirit hovered over the waters. And at Jesus' baptism, he spoke again: "This is my Son" (Matthew 3:17). In both moments, God was beginning a new, extraordinary work—overtaking the chaos and ushering in something entirely new.

And one last fascinating thing you need to know: "waters" represents chaos throughout the Bible. So, in the Genesis account, God's Spirit hovered over the chaos. And in Matthew, as Jesus stood in the Jordan River, his peacemaking presence was colliding with the havoc of humanity.

There's obviously an immense amount of meaning in these moments of baptism as they mirror moments of creation! Let's pause to pull all these threads together.

We'll start with the creation account.

The world began with dark, watery chaos, and the Spirit of God hovered over it like a dove (Genesis 1:2).

Then, God spoke. "And God said . . ." The next verse begins to describe how he entered into the chaos and started bringing order (vv. 3–25).

He created a good, beautiful world characterized by shalom. He created people in his image (v. 27).

After the fall, the world descended back into chaos. And the rest of the story is about how God will infuse his world with shalom once again.

Now let's compare that with the baptism narrative.

Jesus sank into the Jordan River, a picture of turbulent, chaotic waters, and as he rose, the dove appeared (Matthew 3:13–16).

Then, God spoke (v. 17).

God was signaling, *Here is a dawn of a new era, a new creation!*

Afterward, Jesus would begin his ministry and infuse the chaotic world with God's shalom.

Jesus was baptized to "fulfill all righteousness" (v. 15), which involved stepping fully into humanity's chaos, identifying with our brokenness, and beginning the work of healing and setting things right. He wanted to be baptized not because he had sin, but because he came to identify with the sin, pain, and brokenness of the world. Matthew wanted us to see that when Jesus stepped into the Jordan River—and the Spirit of God was there, and the voice of God spoke—Jesus was doing far more than modeling obedience. He was declaring war on the forces of evil and darkness. Baptism was Jesus' way of proclaiming, "I'm coming after you. I'm coming after every last bit of you!"

Before this moment, he hadn't performed any miracles, but once he was anointed by the Spirit, things changed. He went into the wilderness for forty days, where Satan tempted him to live contrary to the will and way of God (Matthew 4:1–11).

Why?

Because Satan knew Jesus' baptism was an act of war. He wanted to derail the movement before it picked up steam.

In the meantime, Herod Antipas had finally had enough of John's preaching. He threw John in jail, all but snuffing out the message of the kingdom. But Jesus refueled the flame when he returned and began to preach, saying, "Repent, for the kingdom of heaven has come near" (Matthew 4:17).

ARE YOU COMING?

In case it isn't clear, all of this revolution talk applies to you—*now.*

Remember that visceral ache we talked about in the beginning of the chapter? The restlessness about the ongoing suffering in this world and how, in our souls, we know things aren't the way they're supposed to be? You and I deeply long for order as we encounter chaos. We want the good King to come and bring his good reign. Somehow—just as Keller described—we sense that we're meant to adore him, belong to him, and serve him.

Well, the moment our King came up out of the waters, he began his campaign against the chaos, and he's still kicking at it today. Now he's turning to you and asking, "Are you coming?"

Jesus' first move in his ministry—immediately following his return from the wilderness—will seem surprising to some. It wasn't a healing, an exorcism, or a sermon to the masses. It was something God has always done: He went looking for partners to join him in bringing heaven here.

Who did Jesus invite first?

Fishermen. Tax collectors. Teenagers. Ordinary people scraping by in forgotten corners of the empire. People like you and me.

Once Jesus gathered his followers, he led them up a hillside and delivered his kingdom manifesto: the Sermon on the Mount.

Do you remember what we said is at the very center of that sermon? The Lord's Prayer! And the core within that, the heartbeat of the whole thing? "Your kingdom come." Jesus put enormous emphasis on it for a reason.

Jesus wasn't simply calling them to believe something; he was calling them to *become* something. Disciples. Apprentices. Citizens of a new kind of kingdom. He'd spend his time on earth creating outposts of heaven wherever he went—pulling heaven and earth back together in himself. He wanted them to learn his ways, take up his life, and join him in carrying heaven's wholeness into earth's brokenness. There was more darkness to fight.

And here's the stunning truth: When you join Jesus in this work, you are bringing heaven here. Not just praying for it. Not just waiting for it. *Bringing it.* With every act of justice and obedience. Every word of forgiveness. Every risk of love. Every time you say yes to his way over your own.

Is that what you had in mind when you said yes to following Jesus and started praying, "Your kingdom come"?

For most of my life, I thought the gospel was about going to heaven after I died. Believe in Jesus, get your sins forgiven, and when this life is over, you'll go to heaven. Maybe you were taught the same. Philosopher Dallas Willard called this approach "the gospel of sin management."[15] It's a truncated gospel.

Yes, forgiveness matters. And yes, life with God after death is part of our hope. But that's not the whole story Jesus came to tell. The whole biblical story is headed toward a renewed heaven and earth.

Again and again, Jesus announced that the goodness and power of heaven wasn't waiting on the other side of death. It was arriving—through him. According to Revelation 21, God's ultimate goal is to reunite heaven and earth, but God's plan for doing so has always involved people. People who not only believe but also embody his will and way. People who aren't just saved but who live as citizens of his kingdom, carrying his life into the world, here and now.

That's what discipleship is. It's learning to live under God's reign—giving your allegiance to King Jesus—and letting his way reshape how you think, speak, work, lead, forgive, and love.

The gospel isn't just about being saved from something; it's about being saved for something. You're not some pet project God is reluctantly trying to fix. You're a partner he's joyfully trying to empower.

A citizen of heaven.

A bringer of the kingdom.

A conduit of his grace and mercy in the world.

This is what you were made for.

This is the revolution you were born to join.

And it doesn't start later. It starts now. It starts here, with the little kingdom you've been given: Your life. Your choices. Your influence.

Of course, that doesn't mean it's all clean and simple. You might be wondering, *If the kingdom of God has come, why is there still cancer? Why is there still injustice, heartbreak, and despair?* Those are valid, vital questions. And we'll explore them in another chapter.

For now, just remember: Jesus never said the kingdom would arrive all at once. He said it was near—meaning, the healing has begun and the invasion is underway. But the war isn't over yet.

The kingdom is breaking in now, and there's much more to come. In the meantime, we live and labor in the tension, with hope.

So, as Jesus is fighting the darkness now—are you coming with him?

If so, the next big question is, How? What would it look like to align your kingdom with his?

It's a whole other conversation. And it's what we'll dive into next.

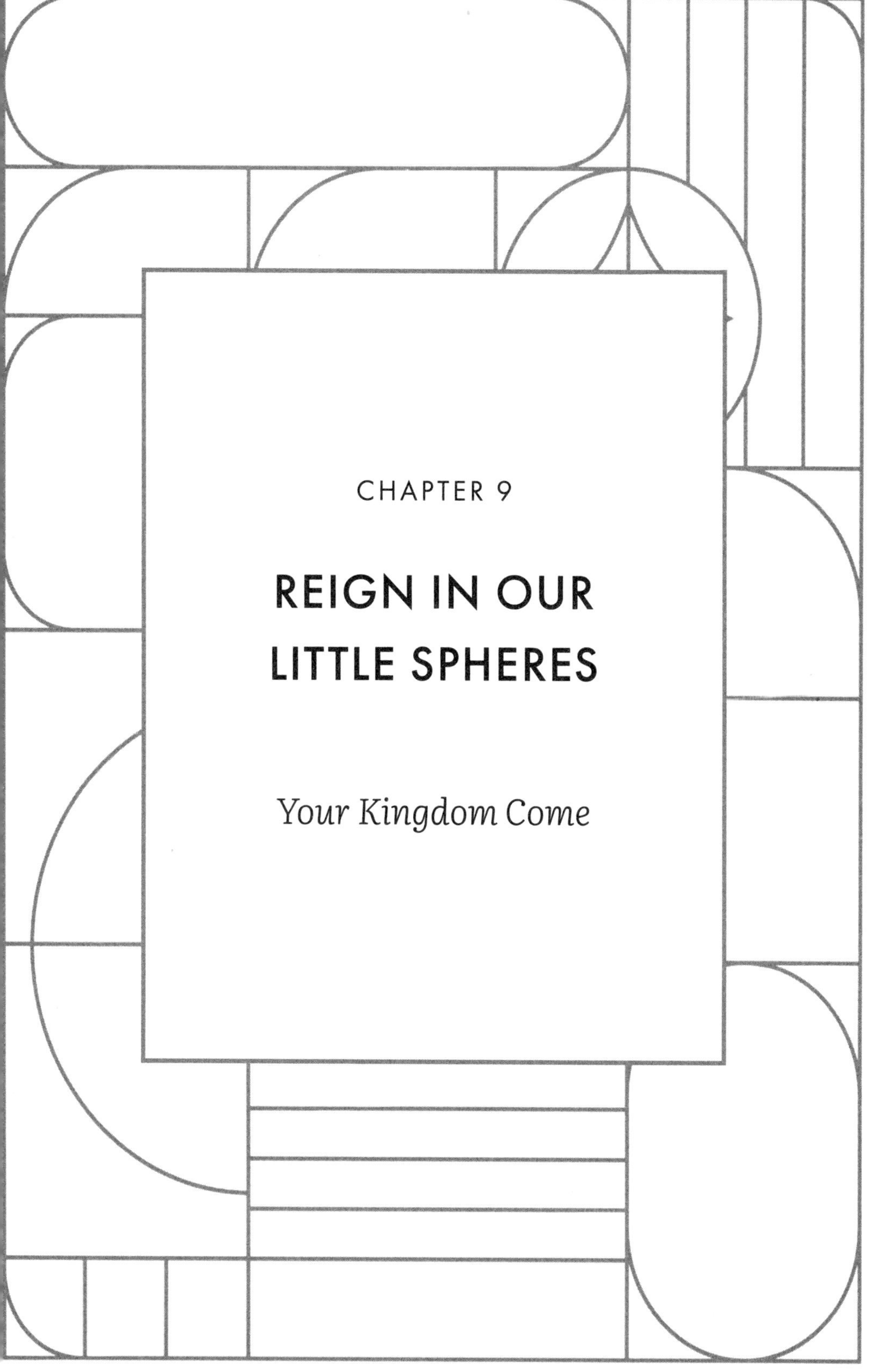

CHAPTER 9

REIGN IN OUR LITTLE SPHERES

Your Kingdom Come

BRAD NELSON

You probably know the name Frank Lloyd Wright, who was one of America's greatest architects. What you may not know is that Wright didn't just design buildings—he built a community.

During a 1949 visit to the University of California at Berkeley, Wright spent the afternoon mostly ignoring faculty and focusing his attention on the architectural students. His parting words to them were, "Come and see us—and bring your sleeping bag."[1]

He was inviting them to visit him and his team at one of his two compounds—Taliesin in Wisconsin or Taliesin West in Arizona.

Some students took him up on the offer. Some even ended up leaving their universities and moving to one of his compounds. Life at Taliesin was nothing like school because Frank Lloyd Wright wasn't just looking for students. He was looking for apprentices.

"Come and see us—and bring your sleeping bag" wasn't a lecture invitation. It was a lifestyle invitation.

Jesus made a remarkably similar one when he said, "Come, follow me" (Matthew 4:19). He wasn't inviting people to attend a Torah seminar or absorb a set of ideas. He was calling them to drop everything, move in, and learn how to live by watching how he lived.

At Taliesin, before apprentices ever touched a drafting board, they might have been assigned to grow food, work in the kitchen, or serve on the grounds crew.[2] This wasn't because Wright was after free labor, but because he believed beauty and design were everywhere. If they couldn't find beauty in the kitchen, they probably wouldn't find it at the drawing board either.

One student, Kelly Oliver, got it. Assigned to kitchen duty, he woke up every morning at 3 a.m. to cook breakfast. But he didn't just bake bread and slap it on the table. He found ways to transform kitchen duty into acts of beauty and creativity, like when he found a fallen walnut tree, cut slabs, oiled them by hand, and foraged pine cones and cranberries to create a display that turned a simple meal into something remarkable.[3]

That's the kind of transformation Frank Lloyd Wright hoped to spark in his apprentices, and it's similar to the kind of life Jesus invites us into as his disciples.

In the last chapter, we defined the kingdom of heaven as the rule and reign of God advancing here on earth—bringing healing and wholeness by pushing out the chaos. We also explored how—in and through Jesus—heaven and earth are being reunited, and how Jesus built a community of apprentices to carry that mission forward.

If we want to become one of his apprentices today, what do we do?

As writers like John Mark Comer have noted, discipleship isn't primarily an educational experience. It's the slow, lifelong process of moving in with the Master, watching how he lives, and slowly letting his way become your way, just like an apprentice does.

Dallas Willard said it best: "The really good news for humanity is that Jesus is now taking students in the master class of life." Is it a class about where you go after you die? No. "It is about living now as his apprentice in kingdom living."[4]

But here's the tension: We didn't follow Jesus through Galilee. We live in a different era and culture. How does the revolution touch the actual contours of our lives—our relationships, routines, responsibilities, and the decisions that ripple out from them? How does that look on a Thursday morning in traffic, meetings, or classrooms? In kitchens, group texts, or checkout lines? Most of us aren't monks or missionaries or pastors. We're just trying to get through today.

You know what, though? That's exactly where the revolution is meant to take root.

Some people think there are two kinds of work—"spiritual work" that matters to God, and everything else. One counts. The other, not so much. This sacred-secular divide isn't just a lie; it's a tragedy, because it's kept countless followers of Jesus from realizing that every dimension of their lives is where heaven is meant to break in.

If you've ever found yourself wondering whether your daily life counts—your project management, your parenting, your coaching, your caring for aging parents—you've felt the weight of it.

But what if it *all* matters? What if your entire life—not just your job, but your habits, relationships, home, and neighborhood—is a little kingdom you've been given to steward?

The revolution in your life doesn't start when you change your career. It starts when you shift your perspective on the life you already have.

THE SACRED-SECULAR DISTORTION

Dallas Willard was the person who helped me grasp the earthshaking significance of Jesus' kingdom message. After my wife, Trisha, and I read *The Divine Conspiracy* in 2002, we'd sit on our kitchen floor late into the night, dreaming about what it might look like to use our lives to bring heaven here. This happened so often, we started calling them "the kitchen-floor conversations." You know the kind I mean—it's the kitchen-floor conversations that make you feel alive.

Those talks lit us up. What could be more exciting than joining God in his work? But at the time, our imagination was limited. To us, "kingdom work" meant "church work." Or maybe nonprofit work. Surely, if we really wanted to bring heaven here, it had to look like ministry. So we both quit our jobs, took temporary ones, and started preparing to become missionaries in China.

Then everything changed. Six months before we were scheduled to leave, my sister's husband was killed in Iraq. Devastated, she moved in with us. China was out. The ministry dream, it seemed, was on hold.

And yet—those months of sitting with my sister in her grief, holding her sorrow, making space for healing—they were sacred. The kitchen table became an altar. The couch, a sanctuary. What we thought was a detour from ministry turned out to be the very center of it.

That's when the illusion of the sacred-secular divide lost its power.

Somewhere along the way, we'd absorbed the false idea that ministry was a category reserved for a select few—pastors, missionaries, church staff. The rest of us? We were just supporting cast.

But Jesus didn't see it that way.

Jesus isn't trying to get more people "into ministry." He's trying to help more people see the ministry already in front of them—in the classroom, the boardroom, the laundry room, or the hospital room. Not to mention the everyday moments of boredom, misunderstandings, arguments, and family get-togethers. When we show up in those spaces with hearts aligned and attuned to God's will and way, *that's* where the kingdom breaks in.

Back in chapter 7, we looked at how God strategically placed the Israelites at the crossroads of the ancient world so the nations passing through could witness a different way of living. He wants to do the same thing with us today. But it doesn't require relocation. The places we inhabit every day—work, neighborhood, gym, school—are cultural crossroads too. We just need to learn to view them that way.

Rabbi Jonathan Sacks once told a story about a brilliant Jewish lawyer who came to him and asked, "Rabbi, how am I to serve God in my daily life? There's nothing religious about being a lawyer."[5]

That question echoes in the hearts of so many people I know—people who love God deeply and quietly wonder if their lives have anything to do with the kingdom of God.

They do.

It's not uncommon for Christians to say, "I want to do something more meaningful with my life. Maybe God is calling me into full-time ministry."

But if you ask that same person, "Are you a follower of Jesus?" the answer is almost always yes. And that's exactly the point.

If you're apprenticing yourself to Jesus, you're already in full-time ministry. The call isn't limited to church, nonprofit, or cause-based work. It extends to every believer in every sphere of life, because God wants partners everywhere—in the arts, media, education, philanthropy, the trades, law enforcement, health care, the home, start-ups, coffee shops, and city councils.

Jesus gave us the Lord's Prayer not to escape ordinary life but to infuse it with meaning. God's kingdom doesn't need more professional Christians. It needs more people who see their ordinary work as a holy offering—who wake up each day with open hands and say, "Use this. Use me."

LEVERAGING OUR LITTLE KINGDOMS

Everyone has a kingdom. As Dallas Willard put it, your kingdom is "the range of your effective will."[6] It's the little sphere where what you say, do, and decide makes a difference—the space you've been entrusted to steward. As the psalmist wrote, "The highest heavens belong to the Lord, but the earth he has given to man" (Psalm 115:16).

Your kingdom is everything you have say over—your time, words, resources, decisions, and relationships. And apprenticeship to Jesus demands a radical rethink of how you relate to all of it.

It's not my house. It's God's.

It's not my money. It's God's.

They're not my kids. They're God's.

You turn toward a new way of thinking, seeing, and behaving. You learn to wake up each morning and ask not, "What do I want done here?" but "God, what do you want done here?"

That's the shift. That's discipleship. That's what it means to align your little kingdom with his.

Sometimes, it starts in small, almost invisible ways.

A teacher may begin each day with a quiet, unspoken prayer: *Dear God, help me to see these students—to really see them. Give me the energy to give them attention where they've been ignored, to offer care where it's been neglected, and to challenge them where they've grown complacent. Help me see what you want to form in them. Help me remember that I don't just teach math—I'm a teacher in the kingdom of heaven. Remind me that your kingdom is coming here too.*

This is how the kingdom comes: not all at once, but in small, faithful choices to live differently. Little by little, your kingdom will reflect more of heaven's priorities, proving that the gospel really is good news for the world.

If you're thinking, *I'm all for this, but it still sounds nebulous*—fair enough. Let's explore three diagnostic questions you can ask to evaluate whether this is happening in your daily life. Each question is related to a calling on your life, so we'll start there.

THREE CALLINGS AND QUESTIONS

"If you're a Christian," wrote Andy Crouch, "you don't have a calling—you have three."[7]

The first is to bear the image of God—the calling we all share, simply by being human. The second is to restore the image of God—joining Jesus in healing what sin has fractured. And the third, what Crouch calls our contingent calling, is the particular way we show up in the world today with our unique gifts, roles, and responsibilities.

As Crouch put it, "If you get the first two right, the third is practically an afterthought."[8]

These three callings give us a framework, but how do we actually live them out? One helpful metaphor is this: Your life is a garden. It's the patch of creation God has entrusted to you—your relationships, work, gifts, and influence. Your first calling is to cultivate that garden—to bear God's image by nurturing your world into fruitfulness. Your second is to redeem what's broken, restoring what sin and selfishness have damaged. And your third is to do both of those things in a way that's uniquely yours.

With that in mind, here are three questions to guide how you steward your life, your little kingdom, for the sake of God's kingdom:

Is this leading to flourishing? *(the calling to bear the image of God)*

Is this redemptive? *(the calling to restore the image of God)*

Am I giving my one sermon? *(the calling to use your unique abilities for God's purposes)*

BEARING GOD'S IMAGE

God created all people to join him as co-rulers, to nurture his good world so it can flourish. Every time we build, design, lead, teach, or innovate, we reflect the Creator of the universe by making something of his world.

Our lives and the spaces where we have influence are like a garden, similar to the garden of Eden God entrusted to Adam and Eve.

If you've ever tried to grow a garden or keep houseplants alive (not exactly my spiritual gift), you know some plants don't thrive in certain conditions—maybe it's too much sun, too little water, relentless bugs, or forgetful owners. Whatever the cause, you can usually tell when something isn't flourishing.

What's true of plants is true of people: We're sensitive to our environments. Most relationships, teams, and communities wilt under neglect, overcontrol, or toxic conditions. Flourishing requires care, attention, and wisdom.

Pursuing flourishing can mean wisely removing restraints to unleash potential—like when a leader steps back in order to empower her team to take initiative, or a teacher scraps the lesson plan when the class gets curious.

Yet flourishing and growth aren't always the same thing. Left unchecked, a garden will become a jungle; weeds will grow and end up diminishing rather than enhancing life. Sometimes the most loving thing a gardener can do is prune. Flourishing isn't freedom to run wild; it's carefully steering toward a particular goal.

For apprentices of Jesus, flourishing isn't necessarily about success; it's about shalom. We've said before that shalom is the deep well-being that comes when our relationships with God, others, ourselves, and creation are rightly ordered. It's wholeness. Harmony. Life as it was meant to be.

So, we might ask, *Is this relationship moving toward wholeness? Is this task contributing to peace? Is this decision cultivating life?*

We also could consider, *Is this home—or team, or neighborhood—flourishing? Is this place becoming more whole because I'm here?*

I have a friend named J. D. who started a medical practice—but not just any practice. J. D. is a lover of trees, an admirer of deep roots and quiet growth. He's also a man who believes people are meant to flourish. So when he launched his clinic, he wasn't thinking only about patient charts and office flow. He was thinking about people in full bloom—both the ones who work there and the ones who receive care.

One of J. D.'s guiding values is *ubuntu*, the South African concept that "a person is a person through other persons."[9] In other words, we can't become fully ourselves unless the people around us are becoming fully themselves too. With that vision in mind, J. D. named the practice Walden, after the place where Henry David Thoreau sought a simpler, more rooted life. The name signals a quiet kind of rebellion: This isn't just a clinic. It's meant to be a place of peace, growth, and mutual flourishing.

You don't have to start a medical practice to live this way. What matters is intention. Maybe it's your classroom, your family, your work team, or even your friend group. What would it look like to see that space as a garden—and to tend it so that everyone in it can thrive? Flourishing doesn't happen by accident. When we start to see ourselves as caretakers of the places and people entrusted to us, everything changes.

As we intentionally nurture our little sphere, we'll be reflecting the image of God.

And wherever we see flourishing, heaven will be breaking in.

RESTORING GOD'S IMAGE

In 2010, scaffolding went up around Rio De Janeiro's Christ the Redeemer Statue for routine maintenance. But under the cover of night, vandals climbed the structure and spray-painted the face of Christ.[10]

In a way, Genesis 3 tells the same story. The image of God was defaced by human rebellion.

That's why our second calling—one entrusted uniquely to the apprentices of Jesus—is to participate in restoring the image of God in the world.

Most of us were taught that the way to do that was by living a "good Christian life"—one with honesty, integrity, and character. In the rough-and-tumble world of exploitative systems, that's no small thing.[11]

But this is expected of all decent people.

What sets Jesus' apprentices apart isn't their commitment to ethics. It's their commitment to redemption.

Redemption is an economic word that means "to buy back." To redeem something means to restore the value that's been lost and return it to its rightful place. To say, "I've been redeemed" is to acknowledge, *Jesus' death bought me back from my slavery to sin and death*, and that's really good news.

But as we saw in the last chapter, that's not where the good news ends. That same self-giving, sacrificial love becomes the template for how Jesus' apprentices join him in restoring the image of God in the world.

So, as we steward our kingdoms, we're not just asking, *Is my kingdom creating flourishing?* We're also asking, *Is my kingdom redemptive?* As Praxis Labs put it, "The redemptive way is creative restoration through sacrifice—to bless others, renew culture, and give of ourselves."[12]

My coauthor has a friend who owns multiple successful businesses. But rather than leveraging those businesses for his own personal gain, he chooses to operate them in light of the kingdom of God. Last year, his companies trained more than eight hundred employees and customers on the biblical principles of finance and generosity. Next year, their goal is to expand that number to two thousand.

What's more, he's made a strategic decision to empower his managers by slowly ceding a controlling stake in the company to them. Ultimately, he intends to entrust it fully to the people who've helped him build it.

He could easily sell the companies he's spent over four decades building and coast for the rest of his life. But he's too deeply committed to using his business to bring heaven here and infiltrate society through redemptive love to do that. "Money can't buy the kind of kingdom influence we've established," he has said.

Not all redemptive action happens in the boardroom, though. Sometimes it happens behind the bread counter.

Catherine worked at a neighborhood bakery, and she didn't just take orders—she knew her customers. She remembered their names and prayed for them. For her, the bakery was holy ground, a little kingdom where she could offer warmth, kindness, and presence.

One day, one of her customers—a widow—mentioned that her car kept breaking down. Catherine had been saving for a new car herself, but immediately, she felt compelled to use her car fund to help the woman in front of her.

"I struggled, giving that money," she said. "But I thought—*I cannot give what I don't have.* So I just gave what I had."

Her selflessness set something in motion. Another customer found out what Catherine had done, went home and told her husband about it, and they decided to buy Catherine a car. When they went to the dealership, the salesperson was so inspired, he jumped in to help out as well.

On the day they surprised Catherine with the car, she broke down in tears. "I knew God had many cars, but I didn't know he had one for me."

Reflecting on the story her generosity had set in motion, Catherine said, "We don't give in order to receive. We give because it is the nature of Jesus Christ. He gave us his life. We have the DNA of Jesus Christ—of giving."[13]

Her story isn't just about a car. It's about a woman who aligned her little kingdom—her job, her money, her presence—with God's redemptive purposes. And in doing so, she ignited a chain reaction of grace.

That's the second calling: not just to reflect God's image, but to restore it—to bring beauty into places of brokenness and participate in heaven's renewal project.

YOUR ONE SERMON

We've said your first calling is to cultivate God's world, and your second is to help restore it. Your third calling is how you uniquely go about doing that with your particular voice.

It's been said that every preacher has one sermon—a single message that comes from the core of who they are. It's a conviction so deep in their bones that it oozes out of them even when they're not preaching. According to his son Leif, Eugene Peterson's one sermon was, "God loves you. God is on your side. He is coming after you. He is relentless."[14] Read Peterson's writings, and you'll find echoes of it everywhere. When Leif was a child, Eugene would whisper those words over him as he slept.

I suspect each one of us also has one sermon—a way we uniquely reflect and announce God's goodness and glory to the world.

For my wife Trisha, that sermon is presence.

She has an almost shocking gift for seeing people. She notices what no one else does. She hears the little things others miss—the quiet details that turn out to be the key that unlocks the deeper reaches of someone's heart. These small, loving acts of recognition elicit so much warmth and appreciation from others, it's like they confirm: *This is the gift she's here to give. This is her one sermon.*

Or there's my friend Steve. He was a pastor for over thirty years, but I met him when he worked in the student ministry office at Cornerstone University. Every guy on campus wanted to be mentored by Steve. He had this sage-like presence and a sixth sense for asking just the right questions, the ones you didn't know you needed until he asked them.

Steve is at his best sitting across the table from someone—one-on-one, heart open, coffee in hand. He's long joked that he has the spiritual gift of meetings. And it's been proven true in one setting after another.

As a pastor, sitting across the table from church people.

As a missionary, across from those he served in China.

As a student ministry leader, across from wide-eyed college students.

He even brought that sage-like presence to the Chick-fil-A restaurant he managed. He called it "pastoring off the grid." That's Steve's one sermon: making space for growth through presence, patience, and curiosity.

Trisha and Steve are so different. But both are showing up every day leveraging their unique gifts.

What about you? Do you know what gift you're here to offer? Do you know what your one sermon is?

Maybe your gift looks more like Trisha's—quiet and perceptive, seeing the unseen.

Maybe it looks more like Steve's—relational and steady, walking with others toward wholeness.

Or maybe it looks entirely different.

Are you good with words? Good. Your community needs someone who can give voice to the longings they feel but don't know how to express.

Are you an encourager? Fantastic. You're surrounded daily by people who are quietly withering for lack of it.

Are you stubborn and hardheaded about doing things right? Perfect. The kingdom needs people like you—who stand up, speak out, and pursue justice with unshakable tenacity.

Maybe you have a knack for finances or technology or the arts. Whatever it is, work at it and offer it as an act of worship. Yield it to God's will and way by asking these three questions:

Is this leading to flourishing?

Is this redemptive?

Am I giving my one sermon?

Run hard in these directions, and you will unleash heaven.

And like Frank Lloyd Wright's apprentices, you don't have to wait to sit down at the drafting table to start designing beauty. Jesus is calling you to begin right where you are.

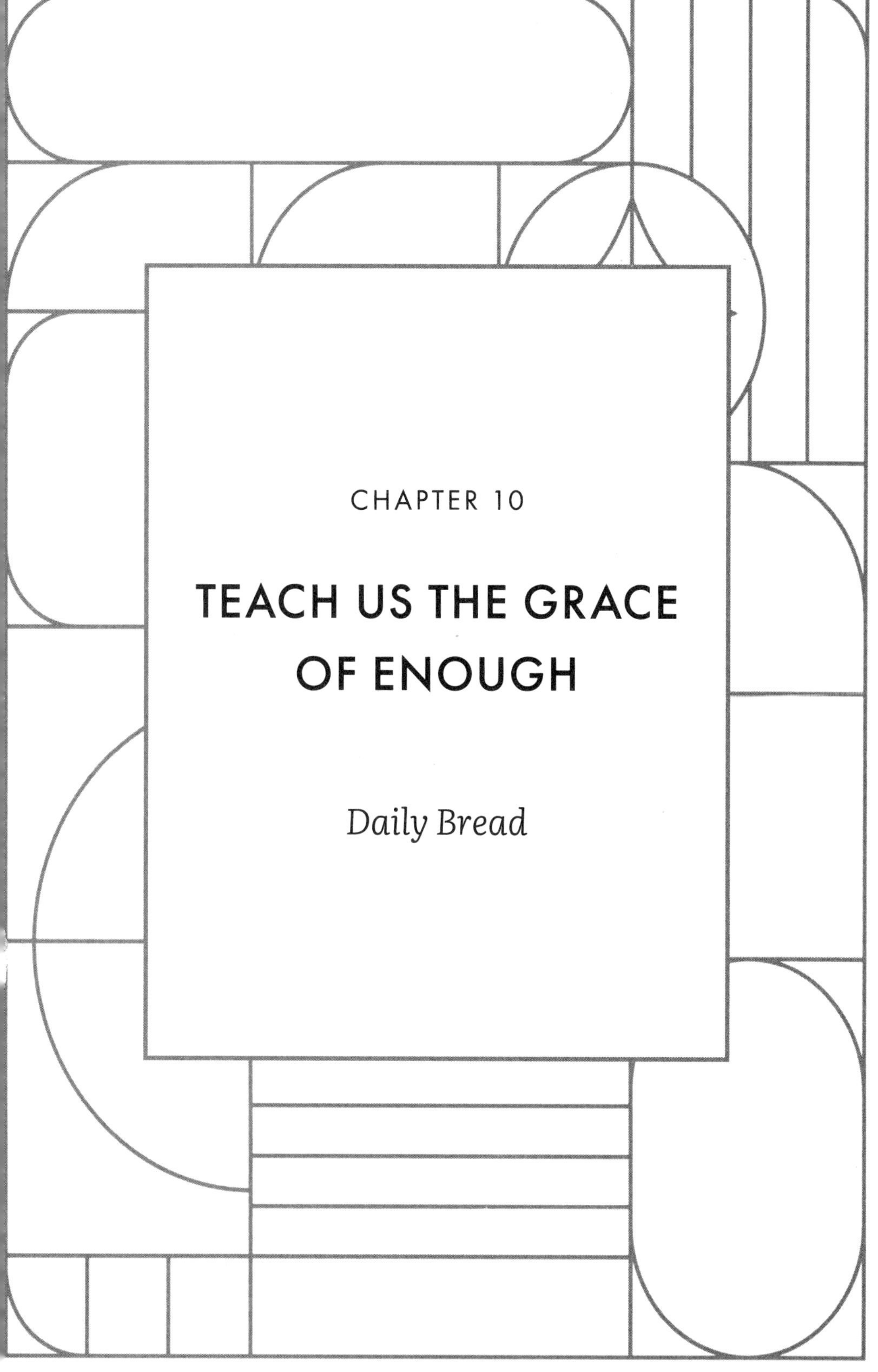

CHAPTER 10

TEACH US THE GRACE OF ENOUGH

Daily Bread

BRAD NELSON

When my oldest daughter turned sixteen, we found ourselves shopping for her first car. My wife and I had offered to cover the up-front cost, and she'd agreed to pay off a portion over time. All the discussions went well—until we started looking at cars.

When I spotted a used Toyota Corolla, I made a pitch. "What about this one? It's in good shape. Great gas mileage. You could drive this well into your post-college years."

But my hard-to-argue-with dad wisdom went unappreciated.

My daughter responded the way she and her sisters often do—by scrambling for their phones and telling me to, "Say it again!" Are they recording these sensible insights for later contemplation? No, dear reader. They are not. They turn them into dad-memes accompanied by the Home Depot theme song.

"Back to the Corolla in question," I gestured.

"*What?* You want me to drive *that*? Ew. No. What is this, *The Beverly Hillbillies*?"

"No. It's a show called *Your Price Range*."

She wanted a BMW. I not-so-patiently explained that, while BMWs are very nice cars, they're not the sort of vehicles Nelson children start out in.

Eventually, she accepted a vehicle far beneath her aesthetic standards.

Nine months and two accidents later, she was forced to sell it for scrap. Then she started shopping for a car on an even tighter budget. Some of the listings she showed me read like cautionary tales:

Needs engine.

Not currently roadworthy.

"Sweetheart," I said. "This one doesn't even have a front bumper."

"I don't care! It runs, doesn't it? Does it *need* one?"

How does a heart shift from BMW to "bumper-free" in the span of nine months?

One word: *need.*

My daughter's experience of *need* reframed the car conversation—from status to function, from what she wanted to what she actually needed. I was proud to see her grow. Though I confess I did want to grab my phone and ask her to "say it again" so I could turn it into a video with *The Beverly Hillbillies* theme music.

She's not alone. We're so formed by the script of consumerism—*you don't have what you need*—that we struggle to tell the difference between what's essential and what's not. And nowhere does this show up more clearly than in our prayers.

N. T. Wright put it like this: "We come to prayer aware of urgent needs, or at least wants. It's tempting to race through the Lord's Prayer as far as 'on earth as it is in heaven,' so that we can take a deep breath and say, 'Now look here: when it comes to daily bread there are some things I simply must have.' Then off we go into a shopping list."[1]

We want a lot of things—and not always the right things or for the right reasons. We're not the first humans to operate this way, of course. In the eighth century BC, God spoke through the prophet Isaiah to ask his people, "Why spend money on what is not bread, and your labor on what does not satisfy? Listen, listen to me, and eat what is good, and you will delight in the richest of fare" (Isaiah 55:2).

Come to me and have your deepest needs met, God was saying. *Receive the spiritual nourishment only I can give.*

ENDING UP STILL HUNGRY

Just like the people of Isaiah's day, we spend an enormous amount of energy chasing what we think will satisfy: wealth, recognition, admiration, and the proverbial "just a little bit more." As we reach and achieve, the sense of fulfillment slips through our fingers. Something always seems to be missing.

Even those who "make it" aren't immune. In his book *The Second Mountain*, David Brooks describes the moment many successful people dread but can't ignore: They "get to the top of the first mountain and taste success, and find it . . . unsatisfying. 'Is this all there is?' Then sense there must be a deeper journey they can take."[2]

Have you ever worked tirelessly for something only to find it didn't deliver what it promised? Or chased after comfort, achievement, or admiration only to end up hungry in a different way? It's not that ambition—or desire, or drive—is wrong. It's that they can send us chasing what can never satisfy.

If you've ever felt the exhaustion of striving, the letdown of arrival, or the ache of "almost," you're not alone. But Jesus invites us to something different. Something deeper. He calls us to come back to the basics—to what really satisfies.

He teaches us to ask for bread.

In the ancient world, bread was more than food. It was shorthand for anything essential. So when we pray for daily bread, we're turning to the Father and saying, *Be my source and my strength for whatever this day holds. Provide what I need to keep going—whether that's groceries or clarity, rest or resolve. Quiet my endless craving for more and teach me the grace of enough. Keep my heart focused on what matters most. And empower me to stay rooted in you as I step into your kingdom work.*

If the first half of the Lord's Prayer anchors us in who God is, why Jesus came, and what our purpose on earth is, the second half is about the things we'll need for the mission of bringing heaven here:

Bread: "Give us this day our daily bread" (Matthew 6:11).

Forgiveness: "Forgive us our debts, as we also have forgiven our debtors" (v. 12).

Deliverance: "Deliver us from evil" (v. 13).

The shift is subtle but significant, and it begins with that line about daily bread, which would have hit Jesus' listeners like a thunderclap.

For them, *daily bread* would've jolted them right back to the desert where God miraculously fed his people with manna every day.

SUFFICIENCY COMES FROM SURRENDER

Like we saw in chapter 3, God didn't lead his people straight to the promised land. Instead, he took them to the wilderness, stripping away all that was comfortable and familiar to expose what was buried in their hearts. God was after more than their liberation. He was after their formation.

Just days into their newfound freedom, the Israelites began complaining, romanticizing aspects of their life in slavery. "If only we had died by the LORD's hand in Egypt! There we sat around pots of meat and ate all the food we wanted, but you have brought us out into this desert to starve this entire assembly to death" (Exodus 16:3).

It's astonishing how quickly hardship reveals the places in our lives where growth is still needed.

Slavery had broken the Israelites' backs, but in the uncertainty of the wilderness, bondage felt safer than freedom. After all, Egypt had systems. Predictability. Stockpiles. Slavery, at least, had a menu. So the people kept grumbling, fixated on all the delectables they'd left behind: "We remember the fish we ate in Egypt at no cost—also the cucumbers, melons, leeks, onions and garlic" (Numbers 11:5).

Freedom meant learning to depend on a God they couldn't control.

So what did God do?

He didn't rebuke them. He provided for them. "I will rain down bread from heaven for you. The people are to go out each day and gather enough for that day. In this way I will test them" (Exodus 16:4).

God's test was simple: *Don't gather more than you need; gather only enough for today. See if you can trust me daily.*

The manna was unlike anything they had ever seen. When it first appeared, they asked, "*Man hu?*"—which is Hebrew for, "What is it?"[3] Eventually, they simply called it *man*, which, linguistically speaking, is how we get the word *manna*. It was a daily reminder that their survival didn't depend on their own control, planning, or stockpiling but on God's pure grace.

There would be a double portion before the Sabbath so they could rest. Otherwise, God's rhythm was clear: *Trust me to provide for you today, then trust that I will again tomorrow.*

The Israelites failed almost immediately—not because they were greedy, but because they were steeped in a particular way of perceiving reality. Some tried to store extra, but it rotted overnight. Others went out on the Sabbath and found nothing.

Why didn't they listen to God?

You'd think after witnessing God's miraculous power with the plagues and the parting of the sea, they'd follow him without hesitation. But after four hundred years in Egypt, they'd been shaped by its worldview, conditioned to believe that security came from control, from having more than enough, from never having to be in need again. They'd developed a scarcity mindset, a distorted vision of the world that says: *Resources are limited; there's only so much to go around. So you'd better get yours before someone else does.*

Near the end of the book of Genesis, one of Egypt's Pharaohs dreamed of seven years of abundance followed by seven years of famine (Genesis 41). Joseph, a Hebrew inmate, interpreted the dream and offered a plan—but it's telling that the guy who owned everything was having nightmares about not having enough.[4]

In the Bible, that's the logic of empire: hoard, store up, secure resources at all costs. Never simply trust that there will be enough tomorrow. Egypt embodied this logic, even building storage cities to guarantee access to future supplies. In Jesus' day, Rome followed a similar script. And—if we're honest—so do we.

Even in a land of plenty, we're nervous about not having enough. In the words of Old Testament scholar Walter Brueggemann, "The central problem of our lives is that we are torn apart by the conflict between our attraction to the good news of God's abundance and the power of our belief in scarcity."[5]

The Israelites felt that same tension. So God led them into a place where their imagination could be rewired. If Egypt trained them that security came from storing up, the desert was where God taught them that sufficiency comes from surrender.

"JUST ENOUGH" TEACHES DEPENDENCE

In Egypt, the Israelites had lived in Goshen—a lush, well-watered region. Moses described it as a kind of garden paradise where people planted seeds and "irrigated [them] by foot as in a vegetable garden" (Deuteronomy 11:10). Watering by foot was one of the perks of living alongside the Nile River. Each year, annual flooding filled the irrigation ditches around the fields. To water their crops, all they had to do was drag their heel through the mud barrier separating their field from the ditch, and the water would rush in. When they were done, they'd just nudge the mud back into place. It was the ancient equivalent of in-ground sprinkling.

Goshen was the definition of abundance. They never had to wonder if there would be enough water tomorrow. According to Lois Tverberg, a teacher on the Jewish roots of Christianity, "The water available from the Nile each year was 30,000 times more plentiful than the yearly rainfall to Israel."[6]

But when the Israelites left Egypt and headed east toward Sinai, the green didn't fade gradually—it stopped abruptly. There's a literal line in the landscape. One moment they stood in the abundance of Goshen; the next, they stepped into the scarcity of the desert.

That line between the green and the brown isn't just a place on a map. It's a place in the human heart.

We all want to have enough, but when is enough . . . enough?

We rarely use the word *enough* to describe what we have. More often, we use it to describe what we lack. Lynne Twist captures this beautifully in *The Soul of Money*:

> For many of us, our first waking thought of the day is "I didn't get enough sleep." The next one is "I don't have enough time." Whether true or not, that thought of *not enough* occurs to us automatically before we even think to question or examine it. We spend most of the hours and the days of our lives hearing, explaining, complaining, or worrying about what we don't have enough of . . . Before we even sit up in bed, before our feet touch the floor, we're already behind, already losing, already lacking something.[7]

Despite being some of the wealthiest people to ever walk the planet, our lives are permeated by the idea of not enough.

But is it true? Are we actually lacking what's essential?

Most of the time, no. It's not our reality but our expectations that are out of sync. Scarcity warps how we see the world.

Years ago, I heard a mom tell the story of their first week fostering a little girl. One afternoon, the mom had made cupcakes, one for each person. But when she went to grab hers, it was gone. So was their foster daughter. After searching the house, they eventually found her hiding in a closet, tears streaming down her face, and both cupcakes stuffed in her mouth. It wasn't greed that motivated her actions but prior neglect and fear.

That's what scarcity does. It tells us to grab what we can while we can, because who knows if there will be more tomorrow? Even when we're safe, even when we're loved, that old script can still run in the background: *take, hide, hoard.*

Scarcity is a sickness of the soul.

So when the Israelites crossed from Goshen's green to Sinai's dust, they were being stripped of the illusion that life is about storing up and taught to live on daily bread—to depend, not stockpile; to trust, not hoard.

It's a tension captured beautifully by one of the most honest prayers in Scripture: "Give me neither poverty nor riches, but give me only my daily bread. Otherwise, I may have too much and disown you and say, 'Who is the LORD?' Or I may become poor and steal, and so dishonor the name of my God" (Proverbs 30:8–9).

Abundance can breed amnesia. Poverty can lead to desperation. But enough—just enough—teaches dependence. It humbles us. It opens our hands. And the wilderness becomes that sacred, disruptive place where what's essential finally comes into focus.

DAILY BREAD IN THE HERE AND NOW

So what does daily bread actually look like in our world?

First, it looks like provision. It's what you need to survive. Not the dream. Just the basics to keep life moving. The fridge with food in it. The mortgage payment that gets paid. The car that starts. The body that functions.

But daily bread also looks like the grace that sustains us on the journey. It's the encouraging text message that comes at just the right moment. A thank-you card reminding you that what you're doing matters. The meal you didn't have to cook. This kind of daily bread doesn't fix everything, but it puts wind in our sails and inspires us to keep going.

Sometimes, daily bread is whatever truly satisfies. A meal around a table with people you love. Using your gifts to bring something good into the world. A moment of laughter that's so cathartic it makes you forget the weight you're carrying. Daily bread is anything that fills you—really fills you—even when life is hard.

And, yes, sometimes daily bread isn't a thing at all but the one who is enough when everything else runs out. But we'll get to that in the next chapter.

In any case, when we pray, "Give us today our daily bread," we'll begin to see daily bread for what it is: provision, grace, and goodness we might have missed otherwise.

NOT MISSING WHAT HE'S GIVING

This is the same kind of message Moses gave the Israelites right before they crossed into the promised land. They'd learned dependence in the wilderness, having "only just enough"; now they'd need to maintain that dependence in a season of abundance.

In Deuteronomy 8:10–11, he essentially said, "When you have eaten and are satisfied, don't forget who gave it to you. Don't let comfort lull you to sleep or a full belly lead to a proud heart. Because if you do, if you start building houses and settling down, watching your finances multiply, you'll be tempted to forget where it came from. You'll think you got here on your own."

If they reminded themselves that everything they had was a gift from God, they could "practice" dependence—which would cultivate gratitude and contentment.

Few people understood this better than the apostle Paul. Writing from Rome "in chains" (Philippians 1:13),[8] he'd discovered the very thing Moses feared the Israelites would forget.

Paul wrote, "I have learned to be *content whatever the circumstances.* I know what it is to be in need, and I know what it is to have plenty. I have learned the secret of being content in any and every situation, whether well fed or hungry, whether living in plenty or in want. I can do everything through him who gives me strength" (Philippians 4:11–13, emphasis added).

It's tempting to press Paul's "I can do everything" into the service of conquering, achieving, and obtaining more of whatever we want. But that's not what he was talking about. Contentment is the posture of heart that says, *I don't need more to be at peace.* It's one of the most powerful antidotes to the when-then thinking that fuels our scarcity-induced anxiety.

When I have more money, then I'll feel secure.
When I achieve more, then I'll feel significant.
When I get ________, then I'll be happy.

But contentment says, No matter my circumstances, I can be at peace—because my strength and well-being come from being connected to Christ.

Paul wasn't claiming that faith in Jesus is a magic formula that effortlessly transforms anxiety into contentment. Rather, his life was marked by certain habits and practices that gradually reshaped his perspective—teaching him to see sufficiency in places where others saw scarcity.

CULTIVATING A CONTENTED HEART

This is an area where ancient wisdom intersects with modern insight. Long before neuroscience gave us the language of cognitive rewiring, Jewish tradition had already developed a practice for reshaping perception through daily gratitude: offering short blessings to God throughout the day.

The idea is to pay attention to all the ways he's providing for you and thank him throughout the day—for the water you drink, the food you eat, the beauty you notice, the warmth you feel, the good news you receive, the family and friends you encounter. It's all a gift, meant to be received with thanksgiving.

It's why Paul instructed believers, "Rejoice always, pray without ceasing, give thanks in all circumstances; for this is the will of God in Christ Jesus for you" (1 Thessalonians 5:16–18 ESV). Thanking God throughout the day is one of the ways we "pray without ceasing."

As Rabbi Jonathan Sacks observed, "The first words we say on waking are *Modeh ani lefanecha,* 'I thank You, living and eternal King.' *We thank before we think.*"[9] Over time, that rhythm of noticing, naming, and honoring grace again and again cultivates a contented heart.

Read through Paul's letters, and you'll see thanks everywhere:

"First, I thank my God through Jesus Christ for all of you" (Romans 1:8).
"I thank my God every time I remember you" (Philippians 1:3).
"How can we thank God enough for you?" (1 Thessalonians 3:9).

Praying for daily bread does the same thing. When we begin each day asking God for provision and end it by thanking him for what showed up, it retrains our attention. We start to see the grace we once overlooked.

It's what cognitive scientists call the Baader-Meinhof phenomenon—or frequency illusion. After buying a car, for instance, you suddenly start spotting the same model everywhere. It's not that there are suddenly more of them on the road. It's that your brain, having deemed the car significant, begins noticing it more often.

It's a shift that's both spiritual and neurological. Brain-imaging studies have shown that anxiety and gratitude cannot occupy the same mental space at the same time; one displaces the other. Gratitude calms the nervous system, reduces stress, and activates regions of the brain associated with peace and well-being (shalom, for those of you who are paying attention!). It's as if God has hardwired our bodies to flourish through dependence and delight.

Of course, the opposite is also true. When we focus on what we lack, it's the only thing we see. Scarcity breeds anxiety. But gratitude breaks the cycle by teaching us to see all the ways God is providing.

Often, it's in the moments when our needs are most apparent that our vision is most clear, and what we might have missed in our abundance becomes unmistakable in our lack.

I've seen this play out in my own life, especially in unexpected moments of lack. One of those moments came during the summer of 2017.

As Hurricane Irma made its way toward Central Florida (where I lived at the time), I foolishly waited to buy a generator, hoping the storm's path would change. It didn't. By the time I made it to the hardware store, there was only one generator left in stock.

It was called—appropriately—the Tailgator.

It cranked out a whopping 700 watts. As the name suggests, it was designed to power a blender at a college tailgate, not to carry a family of five through a natural disaster.

But we made it work.

It ran the coffee maker in the morning, a lamp at night, and—if I woke up every two hours to refuel it—a box fan while we slept. It was far from luxurious or ideal, but it was enough. Even when the power outage continued for eight days, that little generator met our needs. And so it became daily bread for us—a grace that sustained us on the journey.

I smelled like two-cycle engine oil for a month, but I didn't care. I felt nothing but gratitude.

Strange, isn't it? We didn't have everything. But we had enough. And enough can change you.

That's the power of daily bread.

And that's why Jesus says to pray for it.

Don't chase what won't satisfy. Instead, ask your Father to give you what you need. Then watch and give thanks.

Little by little, you'll begin to see his provision everywhere. Let each glimpse pull your heart from the grip of scarcity and open it up to the spaciousness of contentment.

Will God give you everything you want? Maybe not. But shift your focus from that question to what is all around you. If you're paying attention, you'll see—he's already giving you everything you need.

CHAPTER 11

BE OUR ULTIMATE PROVIDER

Daily Bread

BRAD GRAY

In 2016, my wife, Shallon, and I sensed that God wanted me to resign from my job at the church I'd been serving in West Michigan and move our family to Nashville. This was shocking for several reasons. I'd never been to Nashville. We didn't know anybody there. And we'd be moving with no job lined up. We had some money saved, but nothing that would allow us to coast for too long. Everything about the move felt impractical—irresponsible even. It wasn't just the lack of clarity that was unsettling, of course. It was also the lack of provision.

But after two weeks of confirmations that felt so specific it was almost comical, we stood up in front of our congregation and announced, "We're moving to Nashville, and we have no idea why."

Before going public, we'd spent two weeks seeking counsel from mentors, family, and close friends to make sure we weren't being impulsive or naive. God's direction still felt fuzzy, but the collective wisdom of the people we trusted most affirmed it was something we were supposed to do.

I'd love to tell you the rest is history—that we stepped out in faith, moved to Nashville, and immediately found God's blinking lights of clear direction and truckloads of provision.

Not. Even. Close. For the next twelve months, we wandered through agonizing uncertainty. No doors opened. No job materialized. We burned through our savings, and month after painstaking month, I'd look at our bank account and think, *God, are you there? Did we hear you right? How long are we going to have to do this?*

What I thought had been a bold step of faith started feeling more like a daily exercise in survival.

That season taught me something I've never forgotten: The future rarely arrives the way we expect. Most of the time, we can only see the next step. And in that uncertainty, our instinct is to grasp for clarity and control—anything to make the unknown feel less risky. But when Jesus taught us to pray, "Give us this day our daily bread," he was forming us into people who live differently—people who don't demand certainty about the future but trust God in the present.

NO MORE POSING AS SELF-MADE PEOPLE

If we could choose between self-sufficiency and dependence on someone else, we'd choose self-sufficiency every time. We fear the experience of need, doing everything we can to outrun it.

And then the wilderness comes.

Not as punishment, but as mercy. God leads us into wilderness seasons to shatter the illusion that we're self-made, self-sufficient people. In the wilderness, we're forced to trust God as our provider.

Not long after Brad Nelson was born, his dad lost his job during one of the recessions in the early 1980s. When he wasn't out applying for work, he mowed lawns to keep the family afloat. Those days left a deep mark on Nelson's parents. Even thirty years later, his mom still tells the story of opening the cupboards one evening and wondering how on earth she was going to put dinner on the table. Then came a knock at the door. It was some people from the church, standing there with a carload of groceries. "We thought you could use these," they said.

Sometimes an unexpected check would arrive in the mail, often in the exact amount they needed. Other times it was something strange: a surprise tax refund, or a reimbursement for a double payment no one had noticed.

Each time there was a need, provision came from somewhere. Nelson's parents insist it came from some*one*.

What about you? When was the last time you wondered where the money or the food was going to come from?

Maybe it was a stretch of unemployment. Or one of those charming IRS letters informing you that—due to a tax oversight—you owed Uncle Sam an absurd amount of money. Or maybe you've experienced the dreaded triple-whammy: the washer, water heater, and car all breaking down in the same week.

It's in these types of situations that we tend to overreact, imagining futures where a single misstep creates a disastrous domino effect. In this swirl of anxiety, we confuse what *feels* true with what's *actually* true.

This is exactly where the prayer for daily bread meets us—in the tension of ongoing dependence, inviting us to take a posture of radical trust. It's not a prayer that denies fear, but neither does it bow to it.

Fear will tell us that need is an enemy when, in fact, it's a doorway to greater closeness with God. It's how he pulls us nearer and trains us to trust in his provision.

In the wilderness, Moses explained to the Israelites, "He humbled you, causing you to hunger and then feeding you with manna . . . to teach you that man does not live on bread alone but on every word that comes from the mouth of the LORD" (Deuteronomy 8:3).

God wants more than our compliance. He wants to commune with us, and he knows that unless we learn to live one day at a time, we'll never truly trust him.

Eugene Peterson explained it this way: "When we pray for bread we make a decidedly un-American declaration of dependence. . . . We renounce the silly pretentiousness of posing as a self-made person."[1]

To pray "Give us this day our daily bread" is to acknowledge: *I'm not the source. I'm not the provider. It doesn't all depend on me.* It's a prayer designed to help us resist the idolatry of self-reliance and assume a posture of trust.

Something else can keep us from trusting God as our source: turning to other human-level powers instead.

LOOKING TO HEAVEN, NOT ROME, FOR DAILY BREAD

The Roman Empire ran the Mediterranean world in Jesus' day, so the mention of "daily bread" would've made his original listeners think of the Empire's unjust rule over them. In their time, access to bread determined who lived and who died. So Jesus' prayer was meeting them in the shadow of Rome, where bread played a role in manipulation, a fight for control, and survival.

Since 123 BC, the Roman government had been providing a free daily grain allowance—called the *Annona* in Latin—to its citizens living in Rome. This "daily bread" not only ensured food security for the urban population but also served as a political tool to curry favor with the people and maintain control. It was a good deal—if you were Roman. If you weren't? Not so much.

Cunning politicians realized that the fastest way to seize and maintain power was to keep people fed and entertained. So they not only distributed free grain but also sponsored violent spectacles—chariot racing, gladiatorial combat, beast hunts—and the public devoured it all with glee. Well fed and distracted, Roman citizens were more likely to turn a blind eye to injustice and abuse. As long as the Empire met their basic needs and kept the games coming, most believed Rome was doing a good job.

This continued beyond Jesus' time, and by AD 100, the Roman poet Juvenal had seen enough. Disgusted by what the Empire had become, he coined the phrase "bread and circuses."[2] The people, he said, had traded their civic and moral virtue for food and fun.

That's the kind of empire that was ruling "the province" of Judea, where Jesus' original listeners lived.

As Rome prioritized keeping their people fed, it couldn't grow enough grain to keep up with demand.[3] So it took what it needed from provinces like Egypt, Asia, and Judea. Every year, the Empire imported between two and four hundred thousand tons of grain, with approximately seventeen hundred shiploads coming from Egypt alone. Egypt became known as the "breadbasket of Rome."[4] And when supply ran short, Judea, along with other provinces, was forced to make up the difference.

Many of the people listening to Jesus knew what it was like to go hungry so the Romans could eat.

In other words, for Rome to get its daily bread, others had to go without.

The Roman monopoly on grain was so total, it even showed up in their language. They called the Mediterranean Sea *Mare Nostrum*—"Our Sea." Not "ours" in the shared, communal sense. *Ours* as in: *Ours to control. Ours to take.*

But Jesus envisioned a radically different kind of kingdom—one where bread wasn't hoarded, power wasn't used to exploit, and provision wasn't extracted at others' expense. So when he taught his disciples to pray, "Give us this day our daily bread," he wasn't just inviting them to trust God for their needs. He was calling them to resist the illusion that the empire is the source of provision and stability.

In essence: *Don't look to Rome to meet your needs. Look to your Father in heaven.*

You don't have to be under Roman rule to slide into this thinking. The illusion that "someone else will provide for me if I stay in line" didn't die with Caesar; it just got repackaged. Today, we look to all kinds of things for our daily bread—things that promise stability, identity, or comfort, and quietly train us to shift our trust away from our Father in the heavens.

We trust in our bank accounts, believing enough money will insulate us from fear.

We trust in ourselves—our hustle, our competence, our careful planning—thinking we'll earn safety through effort.

We trust in technology, convinced that the right app, the latest device, or the next breakthrough will bring order to our chaos.

We trust in progress—the seductive idea that humanity is always moving up and to the right, that the future is inevitably better than the past.

We even trust in institutions—employers, governments, political parties—hoping that if the right people are in charge, everything will be okay.

But like Rome, these hollow substitutes make promises they can never keep. The Empire says, "We'll take care of you; just don't ask too many questions." The Father says, "I'll take care of you; please come to me daily."

The empire keeps us fed and entertained so we don't notice how hungry our souls have become. The Father invites us to hunger for him, and he promises to satisfy.

By teaching us to pray for our daily bread, Jesus was challenging every system, every story, every instinct that says, *Humans are their own source*—that someone or something other than God can be trusted to meet our deepest needs.

THE REAL BREAD: PRESENCE

Around the same time the Roman poet Juvenal was critiquing the Roman society's obsession with "bread and circuses," a Jewish work now known as 2 Baruch described a new compelling vision: a storehouse of manna in heaven that God had opened to feed the Israelites in the wilderness. The idea was rooted in Psalm 78: "He gave a command to the skies above and opened the doors of the heavens; he rained down manna for the people to eat, he gave them the grain of heaven" (vv. 23–24).

According to 2 Baruch, when the Messiah came, God would open the heavenly storehouse once more.[5] Though it was written after Jesus' death, most scholars agree it reflects the views of many of the Jewish people in

Jesus' day. So when he fed the five thousand, it's no surprise they said, "Surely this is the Prophet who is to come into the world" (John 6:14), and then tried to "make him king by force" (v. 15). A healer, miracle-worker, and source of endless bread would be a powerful ally in a war against Rome.

But Jesus wouldn't play their game. The next day, when the crowds came looking for him, he said, "You are looking for me, not because you saw the signs I performed but because you ate the loaves and had your fill. Do not work for food that spoils, but for food that endures to eternal life, which the Son of Man will give you" (John 6:26–27).

Still, they wanted proof. Moses, they argued, had fed the entire nation for forty years with heavenly bread. Jesus had only done it once (the feeding of the four thousand would come later) with ordinary loaves. So they asked for a sign.

Jesus responded with the least popular—and perhaps most important—teaching of his earthly ministry: "I am the bread of life. Your ancestors ate the manna in the wilderness, yet they died. But here is the bread that comes down from heaven, which anyone may eat and not die. I am the living bread that came down from heaven. Whoever eats this bread will live forever. This bread is my flesh, which I will give for the life of the world" (John 6:48–51).

I'm the real bread.

I'm what your heart is hungry for.

God is providing for your deepest needs through me.

They longed for a deliverer with political might and military power. But the true Messiah stood before them, offering a different kind of freedom, and they didn't want him. Their hearts had been so shaped by Rome's vision of bread—bread as coercive power—that they misplaced their hope.

That refusal to see—to receive—often isn't conscious.

As James K. A. Smith wrote, "Our idolatries are less like conscious decisions to believe a falsehood and more like learned dispositions to hope in what will disappoint."[6]

Again—as we discussed in the last chapter—this is us, pinning our hopes on things that can't satisfy. Reaching, never arriving. Chasing and still ending up hungry. Because, in the end, the human heart longs for more than bread.

It longs for a person. For *the* person.

An aspect of the daily bread Jesus wants us to pray for—the sustenance that meets our core needs—is God's presence: his active and loving energy infusing, shaping, and empowering every step of the journey.

Knowing all this is foundational. But one question critical for our daily moments remains: How do we keep trusting God when the future feels unclear and the pressure mounts?

The answer isn't in gathering more information about the future, but about how we remember the past.

PAST PROVISION IS OUR FUTURE CONFIDENCE

In Isaiah 2, the prophet received a vision of what's to come, a sweeping image of God's kingdom breaking in. The beginning of the account includes a curious phrase: "in the last days" (v. 2).

Most English translations render it "in the latter days" or "in the days to come," referring to the future. But in Hebrew, it's literally "in the behind days."[7] In other words, the future isn't in *front* of us—it's *behind* us. That may sound strange at first, but it makes perfect sense once you understand Isaiah's perspective.

In our modern mindset, the future is something we face and move toward. But for Isaiah, the future is behind us because we are meant to face the past—not to live in it, but to be guided by it. We focus our attention on how God has shown up in our story so we can walk backward—into the unknown future—with greater trust.

In the biblical imagination, turning your back on the past is tantamount to forgetting your story. And when you forget your story, you have no future.

Isaiah understood something we all know but often ignore: The future is fuzzy. Fixating on it too long can make us anxious, frustrated, and overwhelmed. We try to predict what's coming or discern what God might be up to—but most of the time, our guesses don't pan out. A false future disrupts our present peace.

That's why Isaiah invites us to focus our eyes on what we know for sure: God has been faithful in the past, he is present with us now, and he is already waiting for us in the future. And we can walk backward into the future, confident that God has our back.

There's no need to fret about what's coming. Instead, turn and face the past, because in the life of faith, the past isn't dead weight. It's sacred proof of God's faithfulness.

And what did Israel's past entail? A story of provision. A God who rained down bread from heaven, just enough for each day. Isaiah's invitation isn't a nostalgic call to relive the good old days. It's a radical summons to rehearse the future by remembering the past.

Throughout Scripture, God repeatedly commands his people to remember.

Remember how I brought you out of Egypt.

"Remember the days of old" (Deuteronomy 32:7).

"Remember that you were slaves in Egypt" (Deuteronomy 5:15).

In fact, it might surprise you to learn that "remember" is one of the most frequently repeated commands in Scripture.[8] Why?

God knows we can feel overwhelmed by an uncertain future, anxious about where our provision is coming from. So that's exactly where Jesus meets us when he teaches us to pray, "Give us this day our daily bread." He wants us to speak trust in the God who gave manna one day at a time.

Jesus anchors us in the same story Isaiah did: a God whose past provision is our future confidence.

This isn't just an interesting theological insight; it's how trust is built in real life. Trust is about consistency over time. When someone demonstrates their reliability again and again, we feel safe trusting them for what's ahead because they've proven credible in the past.

In his book *The Science of Trust*, legendary psychologist John Gottman says, "The big trust question is, are you there for me?"[9] We answer that question not with grand gestures but through a series of what he calls "sliding door moments." A sliding door moment is any ordinary, daily opportunity to turn toward someone with attention and care.

If you hear your daughter sigh and see her furrow her brow while doing homework, that's a sliding door moment. If you turn toward her and ask, "What's up?"—and then really listen to her—you build trust. If you don't, it's not devastating to the relationship, but it's an opportunity missed. According to Gottman, "these tiny moments of emotional connection form an emotional bank account that gets built over time."[10] The bigger the bank account, the more trust exists, and the more resilient the relationship becomes.

It's the same with God. We build an emotional bank account with him when we remember his faithfulness—daily bread that came right when we needed it. Each memory is another deposit of trust.

That's what happened when we drained our bank account in Nashville. I was filled with anxiety, trying to map the future, and I sensed God say, *Brad, you're facing the wrong direction. Stop obsessing over the future. Turn around and remember. Remember how I've met you. Remember who I've been.*

That moment didn't entirely erase the fear. But in hindsight, I realize I was living the Lord's Prayer without even knowing it. "Give us this day our daily bread" wasn't a theory. It was all we had. Like Israel in the wilderness, all we had was a God who was saying, "I fed you before. I'll feed you again."

And that gave me the courage to keep walking. Not because I knew what the future held—but because I knew the one who had held me in the past.

Even those who don't profess faith recognize the power of this posture. In his famous Stanford commencement address, Steve Jobs said, "You can't connect the dots looking forward; you can only connect them looking backward."[11] He wasn't a Christian, but that insight resonates because it's how God wired the world.

When we stop trying to predict what's ahead and instead remember how he came through, we regain perspective. We see that he's been there the whole time—and he's already waiting up ahead.

I don't know what you're facing today. But if the future feels heavy, try this prayer:

God, you fed me before. Teach me to trust that you'll feed me again. And today—be my bread.

The way forward begins by facing back.

PRAYING IN THE PLURAL

This trust we build in God's provision isn't meant for our comfort alone. It's meant to spill over into the lives of those around us, because when Jesus teaches us to pray for daily bread, he doesn't say *my* bread. He says *our.*

God's provision isn't limited to what we receive. It includes what we give, and that comes through in the plural.

> *Our* Father. *Our* daily bread.
> Forgive *us* as *we* forgive those who sin against *us*.
> Lead *us* not into temptation but deliver *us* from evil.

The communal language is constant.

In the Bible, the word *you* is often plural, but in English, that rarely comes through. Not everyone on the hillside listening to Jesus was poor. Matthew was a tax collector, a man despised not only for collaborating with the Romans but for enriching himself at the expense of his neighbors. And he wasn't the only one with means. Capernaum sat on one of the ancient world's most lucrative trade routes: the International Coastal Highway.[12] In Galilee you'd find Herodians, merchants, soldiers, and well-to-do business owners.

So when Jesus taught them to pray, "Give *us* this day *our* daily bread," it wasn't just a comfort to the hungry; it was a challenge to the full. Sure, there may be bread on my plate, but if my sister's plate is empty, has *our* prayer truly been answered? Which begs the question: What if the bread God placed on *my* plate is the bread he intended for *us*?

Too often, we ask God to act while sitting on our hands, wondering, *When are you going to show up and do something*? I wonder how often the God of the universe thinks, *Funny . . . I was about to ask you the same question.*

Father Ronald Rolheiser once reflected on the phrase many Christians use to close their prayers: "Through Christ our Lord." He wrote, "When we pray 'through Christ' we are praying through the Body of Christ, which includes Jesus, the Eucharist, and the body of believers on earth . . . not only is God in heaven being asked to act; we are charging ourselves, as part of the Body, with some responsibility for answering the prayer."[13]

In other words, to pray the Lord's Prayer with integrity is to volunteer for the answer. It's to say *amen*—and then let our hands, our wallet, our schedule, our choices, and our legs become the prayer.

After returning home from marching with Dr. Martin Luther King Jr. in Selma, Alabama, Rabbi Abraham Joshua Heschel wrote, "For many of us the march from Selma to Montgomery was about protest and prayer. . . . Even without words, our march was worship. I felt my legs were praying."

So when we pray, "Give us this day our daily bread," we aren't just asking for provision. We're volunteering to help distribute it.

None of us can see the future. But we can face it with confidence—not because we've figured it out, but because we remember who has been with us all along. The God who met you before will meet you again. He'll be your bread. He'll be your peace.

And as you receive what you need today, however small, don't forget: If heaven is breaking in through you, you might be someone else's provision.

So take the next faithful step. Trust the God of yesterday. Walk with him today. And become part of his answer for tomorrow.

CHAPTER 12

MAKE US PEOPLE OF RELEASE

Forgive Us Our Debts

BRAD NELSON

One day after a particularly intense family drama, I received a beautiful, handwritten apology from our eight-year-old daughter.

"I'm sorry that I was out of control. Please forgive me."

Then she'd drawn a heart.

My eyes welled up with tears, because parenting is hard. Some days, getting your kids to accomplish basic life skills feels like a superhuman feat. Teaching them the emotional intelligence and humility to apologize and seek forgiveness? A miracle! Her heartfelt apology was evidence that maybe, just maybe, we were getting it right more often than we knew.

I paused momentarily to bask in the glow of that thought, then continued reading.

"You know in the Bible it says do not get mad like you did."

Uh-oh. After that, her heartfelt plea for forgiveness *slash* proof of our parental brilliance took a hard right.

"Feel bad for yourself. You broke one of the Ten Commandments. I know you study and you know the Ten Commandments. I know you know them, cuz that is what God said to the Israelites."

Below that, she'd drawn another heart.

Who *was* this eight-year-old Torah scholar quoting Scripture at me? I didn't want to crush her newfound passion for Old Testament law by pointing out that "Thou shalt not get mad" was not, in fact, one of the Ten Commandments, but I absolutely *loved* that she had the courage to try forgiveness. Doing so had obviously unleashed a wave of competing emotions inside her.

She wanted forgiveness, but she also wanted justice.

Who among us hasn't been there?

Sometimes we think of forgiveness as an admirable, abstract spiritual concept. Other times we know it's far more, and we guard ourselves from the disruptive process of dragging our most painful experiences right up to the surface.

The spouse who cheated.
The coach who abused you.
The friend who betrayed you.
The coworker who threw you under the bus.
The classmate who relished every opportunity to humiliate you.
The family that was supposed to be there for you but let you down over and over.

This is the most difficult and painful part of the Lord's Prayer. Forgiveness stirs up deep emotions and leaves us grappling with what to do with them. A friend of mine once went through such a traumatic professional ordeal that he quit his job and moved his family across the country to recover. Reflecting on his experience, he wrote, "We often don't know what to do with such high emotional and spiritual pain. We default to management tactics to keep it palatable and minimize our wounds to help them feel survivable."[1]

Do you know what your go-to management tactics are? Maybe you're the type who keeps insanely busy to sidestep your feelings. Or perhaps you scroll, snack, shop, or bourbon your emotions away. Oddly enough, my preferred form of emotional suppression is cleaning. If you've never shut out your feelings by washing a sink full of dishes in a blind rage, then you, my friend, haven't lived.

While avoiding, minimizing, managing, or suppressing your pain might help you survive, these things won't help you thrive. In fact, as we mature, we discover an unpleasant but transformative truth: The defense mechanisms that once kept us safe are the biggest barriers to our continued growth. Eventually, life throws down the gauntlet: Either you deal with the pain or the pain deals with you.

Jesus invites us to process, integrate, and transform the pain into something generative and life-giving. And he does it through forgiveness.

The Lord's Prayer makes the audacious claim that forgiveness is such a vital component of the kingdom of heaven, it demands daily attention.

The big problem is, forgiveness is messy, and it's not always clear what it entails.

Does forgiveness mean forgetting?

Does it mean forfeiting your right to justice?

Does it mean the person who wronged you gets off scot-free?

Dr. Robert Enright, a pioneer in the scientific study of forgiveness, found that "one hundred percent of the problems people have with forgiveness are based on a misunderstanding of the concept."[2]

Facing an unpleasant task without a clear understanding of what you're up against is paralyzing. Imagine someone with a debilitating medical condition that no doctor has been able to diagnose. How do they feel?

Helpless.

Hopeless.

Stuck in neutral.

Now imagine how they feel when a doctor comes along and says, "Ah! I know what this is. You have _______. Here's what we need to do." Naming the disease doesn't solve the problem, but it frees up an enormous amount of energy to face the difficult road ahead.

Understanding Jesus' words in their original context will not only clarify what forgiveness is and isn't; it will help you understand why it's so hard and offer practical insight about what the path ahead looks like. While forgiving people won't become easier, you will be able to walk the path with new confidence.

You'll also be encouraged to see that Jesus isn't asking you to do something he hasn't already done himself. He set the example, and now he beckons, "Follow me."

My hope is you'll have the courage not only to try forgiveness but to join Jesus in bringing heaven here by making it part of your daily life.[3]

FORGIVENESS AS RELEASE

Matthew 6:12 reads, "Forgive us our debts, as we also have forgiven our debtors." The word *forgive* comes from the Greek word *aphiēmi*, meaning "to let go" or "to release."[4] In the first century, financial debt was the primary metaphor for what occurs when we harm another person: We owe them a debt. Forgiveness, then, means releasing someone from the debt they owe because of the hurt they caused. In essence, you forfeit your right to get even by handing them over to God.[5]

You can release someone without condoning what they did to you. You can forgive without minimizing the damage or pretending "it wasn't so bad." In fact, forgiveness insists, "This matters, and it matters enough to hold you accountable." That takes spine.

Yet many of us grew up with the phrase "forgive and forget" stitched into our moral fabric. It sounds noble, but it's a fallacy. Trying to forget the pain we've experienced is like trying to breathe underwater. We're simply not designed to operate that way.

When we try to forget painful experiences—by ignoring, numbing, suppressing, or repressing—the body remembers.[6] This is why a combat veteran can be jolted by the sound of an engine backfiring or why a scent can resurrect a memory we thought was long gone. Our bodies have stored the pain as implicit memory, etched into our very sinews; it's no wonder we can sense something pressing against a bruise as if to say, *I'm still here. This still hurts*. Pain won't let us forget.

So forgiveness doesn't try to erase the past. It offers a way to transform it.

This doesn't always mean reconciliation. Some harm is irreparable, and restoring the relationship may not be possible or even wise, and that's okay. If you seek to restore the relationship, forgiveness might require setting and guarding appropriate boundaries to prevent further harm.

Forgiveness does not require an apology or consent from someone. It is a one-way street. You can forgive someone who's dead, someone who has no remorse, or even someone who doesn't believe they've done anything wrong.

Although forgiveness means forfeiting your right to get even, it doesn't mean forfeiting your right to justice—actions have consequences, and forgiveness doesn't turn a blind eye to the legal, financial, or relational implications of wrongdoing. You can forgive someone and still require them to make restitution.

We possess an innate longing for justice, but while justice might satisfy our idea of what's right or fair, it can't undo the past. Forgiveness helps us accept that what's lost is lost, and then it invites us to ask a courageous question: "How do I cultivate a life of meaning and possibility given that this is now part of my story?"

Finding the strength to ask and live out that question takes time, and we'll explore that in the next chapter. For now, let's get a deeper understanding of what it means when Jesus speaks of forgiveness as release.

RELEASE VERSUS BONDAGE

Release is a major theme in the Hebrew Scriptures, one that would have resonated with Jesus' audience on multiple levels.

For starters, release is at the heart of the exodus story. After releasing his people from their bondage in Egypt, God brought them to Mount Sinai and made a covenant with them, commissioning them to become a people of release. One section of the covenant includes specific instructions for what is known as the Year of Jubilee: "Consecrate the fiftieth year and proclaim liberty throughout the land to all its inhabitants. It shall be a jubilee for you; each of you is to return to your family property and to your own clan" (Leviticus 25:10).

Jubilee was a big deal. Back then, if you couldn't pay your bills, you might have to sell your family estate or even become a slave to settle your debts! But during Jubilee, debts were wiped out, slaves were set free, and any family property that had been lost through sale was restored to its ancestral owners. Jubilee was God's way of saying, "Release is so important to me, I want you to mark it on your calendar."

What's even more telling is that sometime between the third and second century BC, a group of Jewish scholars were commissioned to translate the Hebrew Bible into Greek (known as the Septuagint). When they came to Leviticus 25, they translated the Hebrew word for *jubilee* with the Greek word *aphiēmi*, meaning "release." Jubilee was literally "the year of release."[7]

While historians debate whether the Israelites actually practiced Jubilee, one thing is clear: God expected them to. Moses spelled out the terms of the covenant in Deuteronomy 28 with a clear message: Essentially, "Obey, and you'll flourish. Don't, and things are going to get bad."

Here's a sampling of the words Moses used to describe just how bad things would get:

No respite.
No rest.
An anxious mind.
Weary eyes.
A despairing heart.
Constant suspense.
Hearts filled with terror.

And, worst of all, *back to Egypt* (Deuteronomy 28:64–68).

Friends, exile is the exodus undone. When we refuse to release others, we put ourselves back in bondage.

FORGIVENESS, EXILE, AND THE KINGDOM OF GOD

By the time Jesus began his ministry, most Jews believed they were living out those curses under the Roman occupation. Yet they had reason to hope that one day, Israel's Messiah would come to their rescue announcing a message of release. They clung to the prophets' promises, such as Isaiah 61:1: "The Lord has anointed me to proclaim good news to the poor. He has sent me to bind up the brokenhearted, to proclaim freedom for the captives and release from darkness for the prisoners."

Isaiah 61 describes the ultimate reversal of fortunes, and just like the Jubilee texts, the chapter's beating heart is the word *release*. It was the message Jesus' audience was most desperate to hear. And it was the exact passage Jesus chose to read in his synagogue sermon in Nazareth at the beginning of his ministry.

It created quite a stir.

When Jesus finished reading, "he rolled up the scroll, gave it back to the attendant and sat down. The eyes of everyone in the synagogue were fastened on him. He began by saying to them, 'Today this scripture is fulfilled in your hearing'" (Luke 4:20–21).

That's what you call a first-century mic drop. Technically, in Hebrew, it would be called a "scroll slam," but that's neither here nor there.

Jesus was claiming that, in and through him, God's great release was finally underway![8] And he went on to demonstrate it by the way he lived. His healings released people from sickness. By casting out demons, he released people from evil. Every time he shared a meal with sinners and tax collectors, he released them from exclusion and isolation. He even claimed, "I want you to know that the Son of Man has authority on earth to forgive [or release, *aphiēmi*] sins" (Matthew 9:6, emphasis added).

To a first-century Jew, those words were code for the new exodus.[9]

When God's anointed one shows up and starts releasing people from their sins, it unleashes the kind of radical healing of relationships that can only be described as heaven on earth: the kingdom of God!

When you forgive, it's proof that heaven is invading earth, and your life is the front line of the invasion.

SETTING THE PRISONERS FREE

Abraham Twerski was a Hasidic rabbi and psychiatrist specializing in substance abuse. One day while attending an AA meeting, he overheard a participant utter words that have since entered our cultural lexicon as a kind of proverb: "Harboring a resentment is allowing someone you don't like to live inside your head without paying rent."[10]

Does it ever feel like there's not just a person but a whole apartment complex of people living inside your head? Honestly, when was the last time you overheard yourself telling someone off in the shower? Giving someone a piece of your mind while driving all by your lonesome? Does the mere mention of someone's name trigger an eye roll and a contemptuous, "Ugh. I can't stand that guy." Sometimes I'll be going about my business, not thinking of anything in particular, and out of nowhere, I'll recall someone's face and the hurtful words they spoke. When it happens, it's like I can still feel where the knife went in.

If any of these moments resonate with you, there's a good chance someone's living in your head.

We convince ourselves that by holding on to the anger, we're somehow holding the perpetrator accountable. Locked in the cell of our consciousness, they can never escape our wrath! We're "free" to visit anytime, day or night, and spew our righteous venom.

In reality, though, the only person we're hurting is ourselves.

If you're holding on to hurt, it won't be long before that hostility and anger start echoing through your life, coloring everything you experience.

In *The Book of Forgiving*, Ben Bosinger describes how his abusive father permeated his consciousness, saying, "I realized that I was carrying him with me everywhere I went, into every intimate relationship, and even into my own parenting. It was this more than anything, I think, that made me simply turn my motorcycle up his driveway one afternoon. I was sick and tired of being sick and tired. The pain of constantly carrying him with me was finally greater than the pain of the beatings I took as a child. Something had to give."[11]

The heartbreaking truth about unforgiveness is that what we hold on to holds on to us.

Forgiveness whispers:

Is there pain you're keeping in circulation by refusing to release it?

Are you holding on to something that's keeping you chained to a particular person or event?

Are you harboring resentments that are slowly eating away at you from the inside?

Who and what do you need to release?

If you're sick and tired of being sick and tired, Jesus invites you to become a person of release and discover the counterintuitive truth that we free ourselves by freeing others.

CONFESSION AND RELEASE

It's one thing to forgive, but what about when you're the one needing forgiveness? Jesus' phrasing cuts both ways: "Forgive us our debts, as we also have forgiven our debtors" (Matthew 6:12).

One of the most soul-crushing lines from my daughter's handwritten apology was, "When you burst out in madness, it just makes me feel like you hate me." Even now, a decade later, reading those words wrecks me. I love her fiercely, and the thought that my anger did that to her eight-year-old heart is deeply convicting.

But that's the messy work of forgiveness.

Sometimes, you go looking for an apology and what you get instead is an accusation. Forgiveness forces you to face those parts of yourself you'd rather ignore and step into the murky space between what was done to you and what you did to someone else. Becoming a person of release requires the humility to own up to those moments when you're the one who's in debt and in need of release. It's impossible to pray, "Forgive us our debts, as we also have forgiven our debtors," without confessing our wrongs.

That's how we clear the air with those we've hurt. If the thought of confessing your sins on a daily basis sounds cringeworthy, consider these words from Eugene Peterson: "God does not deal with sin by ridding our lives of it as if it were a germ, or mice in the attic. God does not deal with sin by amputation as if it were a gangrenous leg, leaving us crippled, holiness on a crutch. God deals with sin by forgiving us, and when he forgives us there is more of us, not less."[12]

Confession whispers:

Am I the one living rent-free in someone else's head?

Is there pain I've unleashed that I've not yet named and owned?

Could humbling myself be the key to someone else's healing?

Where do I need to be released?

Like I said, the path ahead isn't easy, but in the kingdom of heaven, the things you think will kill you often end up saving you—and spitting you out the other side a larger person.

Also, pain festers when it's left unaddressed. Like magma beneath the surface of the earth, the pressure builds, until it erupts, leaving behind smoldering wreckage. If we don't deal with it, we pass it along—to our kids, our coworkers, our spouses, our friends, even our future selves.

That's why praying, "Forgive us our debts, as we also have forgiven our debtors," is a form of early detection and preventive soul care. The daily rhythm is what keeps wounds from hardening. It invites reflection before resentment calcifies.

My friend Jeff recently said something to me that I didn't want to hear but needed to. He pointed out that I have a pattern in relationships: I wait too long to say what I want or need. At first, I brush things off or convince myself I don't need much at all. It's a form of self-protection: pretending I'm fine so I don't risk being disappointed.

But, as Jeff gently reminded me, we're needs-based creatures. You can suppress your needs for only so long before things start to corrode from the inside out.

By the time I finally speak up, he said, the need has usually grown so large—so emotionally loaded—that no one could realistically meet it. It becomes overwhelming. His challenge to me was simple, but wise: Name what you need sooner, when it's still small, clear, and manageable.

Forgiveness is similar. It can feel so heavy that we put it off, telling ourselves we're not ready. But in the waiting, the hurt grows. The roots sink deeper. And by the time we finally confront it, it's no longer a small ask. It's a mountain.

Maybe that's why Jesus invites us to pray about forgiveness every single day. Not because we'll always feel ready, but because we can't afford to let pain take root. We need to deal with the small stuff while it's still small.

What if today when you pray, "Forgive us our debts, as we also have forgiven our debtors," you paused briefly to review the last twenty-four hours and ask:

Did anyone hurt me today, even just a little?

Did I hurt anyone today, even just a little?

If so, name it.

Then do what you can to respond: pray, confess, reach out, release. The action doesn't have to be big. Just don't wait too long.

No more suppressing your pain or letting anger echo through your life. No more living in bondage, obsessing over "what they did." In his kingdom, we can free ourselves by freeing others and unleash radical healing. We can bring heaven to earth and cultivate a life of meaning and possibility, no matter what wounds or wrongs we bear. This is the invitation of the Lord's Prayer, the vision Jesus sets before us.

Next comes the question, *How in the world do we actually live this out day after day?*

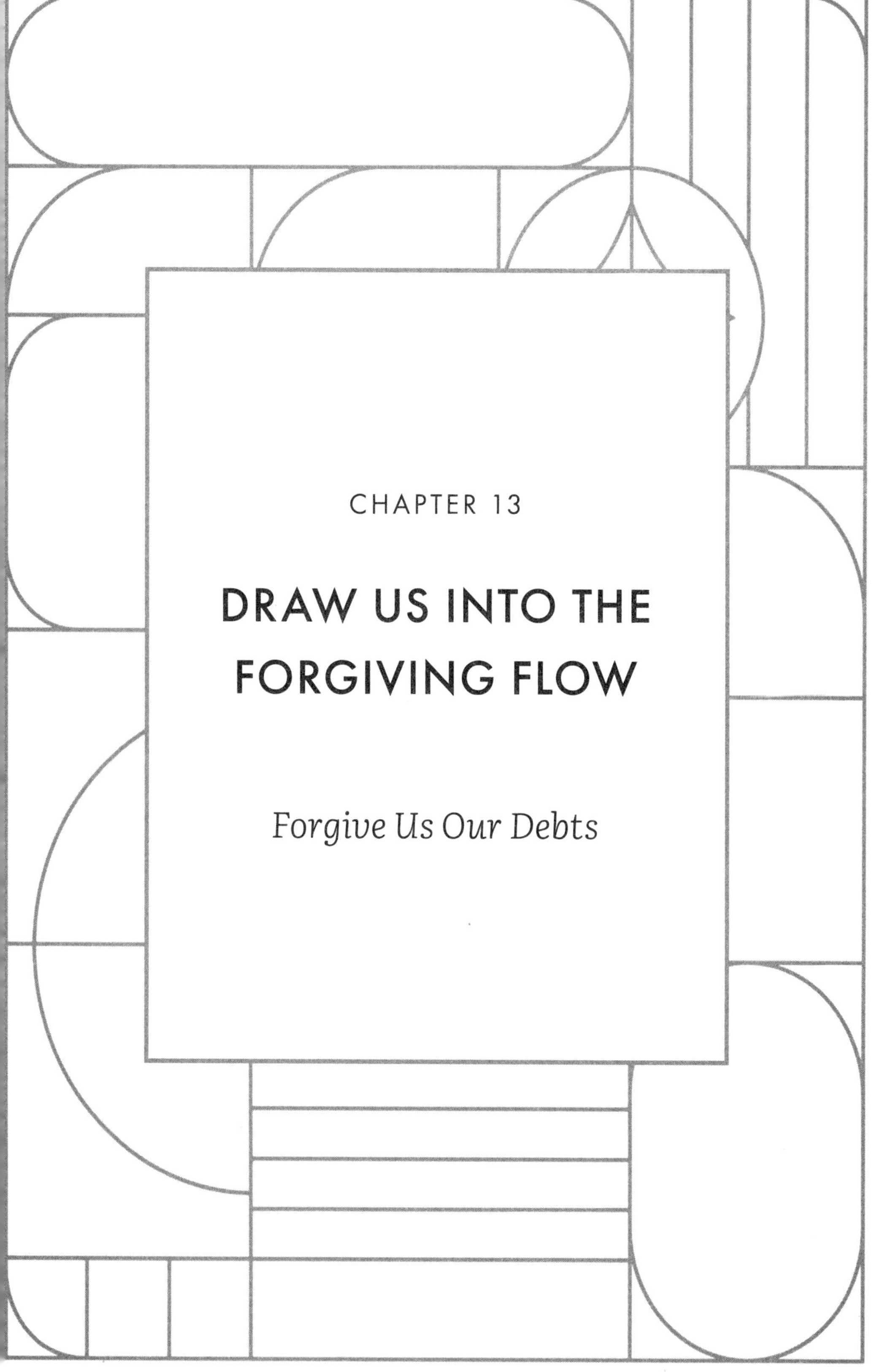

CHAPTER 13

DRAW US INTO THE FORGIVING FLOW

Forgive Us Our Debts

BRAD GRAY

In 2008, British television presenter and author Jeremy Clarkson purchased a thousand-acre farm in Oxfordshire. After the local farmer he'd been employing to run the farm retired, Clarkson thought, *I'll just do it myself. How hard can it be?*

His logic?

"Man has been farming for 12,000 years. So, I figured it must be in our DNA by now. You put seeds in the ground, weather happens and food grows. Easy."[1]

As my Southern friends in Nashville might say, *Bless his heart.*

After a year of backbreaking toil, Jeremy's farm earned him a "profit" of £144—the equivalent of $184. It turns out, farming isn't easy after all. It's an endless cycle of preparing, planting, fertilizing, fixing, spraying, waiting, harvesting, and hoping for the right weather. Not only is farming dangerous and discouraging; at times it's downright impossible. You can do everything right, and something beyond your control—bad weather, a barley-eating beetle, or a global pandemic—can ruin everything.

Yet Clarkson called it the happiest he'd ever been at work. The difficult process of farming was forging an unexpected bond, connecting him more deeply to the land, the food he ate, and the people he cared about.

I tell you all this because forgiveness is a lot like farming. You can do everything right, and things can still go wrong.

You can know what forgiveness is and isn't.

You can know who you need to forgive.

You can even want to forgive them, and still it can feel impossible.

It's not as simple as saying some words, letting a little time pass, and *voilà!*—bygones are suddenly bygones. It's difficult, demanding work. According to the late pastor and author Tim Keller, forgiveness is hard because choosing "to refrain from lashing out at someone when you want to do so with all your being is agony. It is a form of suffering . . . but it is a death that leads to resurrection instead of the lifelong living death of bitterness and cynicism."[2]

In other words, it's hard, but it's worth it.

And it's a way we practice the resurrection.

The key is to develop resilience when we face the difficult work of forgiveness, to stay connected to the source, and to join "the forgiving flow."

IT'S A PROCESS

Peter once asked Jesus, "Lord, how many times shall I forgive my brother or sister who sins against me? Up to seven times?" (Matthew 18:21). Forgiving someone seven times would have been considered extremely generous. Rabbinic tradition later taught that "if a man commits a transgression, the first, second, and third time he is forgiven, the fourth time he is not."[3]

Perhaps Peter was looking for a number. Or maybe he was looking for more than a number. In the Bible, the number seven symbolizes completeness. In essence, Peter was asking Jesus, "What does real, complete forgiveness look like?"

Jesus responded by saying, "I tell you, not seven times, but seventy-seven times" (Matthew 18:22).

Seventy-seven isn't a random number designed to exaggerate Jesus' meaning. It's a deliberate reference to a story from Genesis. Jesus was engaging Peter in what was known as *remez*.

In Hebrew, *remez* means "hint." In a culture where Jewish men, women, and children had large portions of the Hebrew Scriptures committed to memory, Jewish sages and rabbis could make even a small reference to a text and know their audience would not only catch the "hint" but also import the context of the passage into the present conversation.[4]

It's a little like quoting an epic movie line in a conversation or singing a popular song lyric in an everyday moment. It only takes a few words for people to know immediately what you're referring to and why the context of the original work connects with the present situation.

Jesus' response to Peter worked the same way. By making a reference to *seventy-seven times* after mentioning *seven*, Jesus was pointing to a story about Lamech, who was a descendant of Cain, the Bible's first murderer. Apparently, the apple hadn't fallen far from the tree. Lamech also had committed murder—and then written a song about it and performed it for his wives.

As you do.

Genesis tells us, "Lamech said to his wives, 'Adah and Zillah listen to me . . . I have killed a man for wounding me, a young man for injuring me. If Cain is avenged *seven* times, then Lamech *seventy-seven times*'" (4:23–24, emphasis added).[5]

By pulling the Lamech story into the discussion about forgiveness, Jesus answered Peter's question in a powerful and unexpected way. He was calling Peter to pursue forgiveness with the same kind of relentless passion that drove Lamech to seek vengeance.[6] In the same way that Lamech's desire for vengeance went beyond a single act, true forgiveness is an ongoing process—it's not fulfilled in a single moment.

This is why Jesus teaches us to make forgiveness part of our daily prayers. "Forgiveness," wrote Henri Nouwen, "is the name of love practiced among people who love poorly. The hard truth is that all people love poorly. We need to forgive and be forgiven every day, every hour increasingly. That is the great work of love among the fellowship of the weak that is the human family."[7]

Without the ongoing process of forgiveness, human relationships would go up in flames.

But I believe there is another reason we need to pray for forgiveness daily, and it's the fact that some wounds take a long time to heal. According to Dr. Everett Worthington Jr., a renowned forgiveness researcher, certain kinds of pain require special effort to forgive—such as repeated offenses from the same person, catastrophic events, or the ongoing wounds of trauma and abuse.[8]

You can't rush forgiveness. It's more like grief; it comes in waves, and it comes when it comes. There are some wounds we'll have to pray for the strength to forgive over and over and over again.

There likely will be moments when you catch yourself thinking, *God, I want to forgive, but I just can't seem to.*

God, will I ever be able to forgive that person?

I thought I'd already put this behind me! Why am I still feeling this?

Having these thoughts doesn't mean you're doing it badly. It just means that forgiveness is a process, and you're in it.

I know this all too well.

Recently, I walked through one of the most painful experiences of my life. Someone very close betrayed me in a way I never could've imagined. It's been the darkest, most disorienting breach of trust I've ever known, and forgiveness hasn't come easily.

I've had a horrible time stomaching it. I've given my life to following Jesus and living out his prayer, but this—this has been one of the hardest acts of obedience I've ever attempted. That's what makes this line of the prayer so difficult. We know what we're called to do. But knowing what you're called to do doesn't automatically change how you feel about doing it.

And in this case, forgiveness hasn't led to reconciliation. There hasn't been a warm reunion. No bow tied on the end of the story. I'm still in process: praying, struggling, surrendering. It's slow. It's hard. And I know no other way to sustain such challenging work than to just keep showing up, because that's what faithfulness looks like right now.

But here's the catch: We don't have to show up alone.

THE SOURCE

When I lived in Israel, I spent a year studying at Jerusalem University College, the quintessential "classroom without walls" located within the Old City. It's one part Jesus, one part graduate school, and one part Indiana Jones. I learned more about the Bible by walking the land than I ever could've in a typical classroom. After all, geography is the ever-present character in every Bible story.

In the late fourth century AD, Saint Jerome made this same observation: "Five gospels record the life of Jesus. Four you will find in books and the one you will find in the land they call Holy. Read the fifth gospel and the world of the four will open to you."[9]

Saint Jerome was right. When you understand the land, it opens up a world of biblical wisdom and insight. For example, understanding how Israel's three largest bodies of water—the Jordan River, the Sea of Galilee, and the Dead Sea—connect transformed my understanding of Jesus' words on forgiveness in the Lord's Prayer.

Compared to the Mississippi, the Jordan is tiny, but it's Israel's only major river system. In Hebrew, the Jordan River is called *Yarden*, which means "descender." Its headwaters form at the base of Mount Hermon in northern Israel and then "descend" twenty-five miles into the Sea of Galilee. After flowing through the Sea of Galilee, it descends another 130 miles to the south until it empties into the Dead Sea, the lowest point on earth.[10]

While the Sea of Galilee teems with life—migratory birds, a thriving fishing industry, the largest source of freshwater in the land—the Dead Sea is barren. It has no birds or fish, only bacteria, algae, and minerals. Both are fed by the same source, but only one supports and sustains life. Why?

They each do something different with what they receive. The Sea of Galilee passes on what it receives from the Jordan, but the Dead Sea hoards every drop that comes its way. In the words of Rabbi Jonathan Sacks, "To receive without reciprocating is a kind of death. To live is to give."[11]

The Lord's Prayer implies a similar relationship with forgiveness. Forgiveness has a Source. It comes from our Father in the heavens, flows into our lives through Jesus' work on the cross, and then "carves our lives into a channel through which the healing stream of spirit can flow to a world in need."[12] By staying connected to the Source, we can do what feels impossible because we're not operating in our own power. We're cooperating with his, and it only works when what flows to us also flows through us.

THE FLOW

The traditional ending of the Lord's Prayer wasn't added until sometime in the fourth or fifth century AD. It originally ended with the words, "If you forgive other people when they sin against you, your heavenly Father will also forgive you. But if you do not forgive others their sins, your Father will not forgive your sins" (Matthew 6:14–15).

Forgiveness is such a pivotal part of bringing heaven here that Jesus addressed it twice. He was emphasizing the intimate connection between the forgiveness God extends to us and the forgiveness we extend—or withhold—from others.

One of the key principles for interpreting Scripture in Jesus' day was a technique known as *gezerah shavah*, or "to cut equally." Sages and rabbis would connect two unrelated passages from the Hebrew Scriptures based on a key word or phrase that appears in both texts, then they would gain a new understanding of the passages in light of one another.

For example, when Jesus said in Matthew 22:37 that the greatest commandment in the Law was to "love the Lord your God with all your heart and with all your soul and with all your mind," he was quoting Deuteronomy 6:5. When he said, "And the second is like it: 'Love your neighbor as yourself,'" (v. 39) he was quoting Leviticus 19:18. Both passages include a Hebrew word that appears only a handful of times in the Hebrew Scriptures—*ve'ahavta*, which means "and you shall love."[13] By linking these two passages, Jesus was identifying this critical word and "cutting the passages equally." His point was, we love God when we love our neighbors well, and we love our neighbors when we love God well. They go hand in hand.

The Lord's Prayer teaches that the same is true for forgiveness. Forgiven people forgive people.

If, however, we believe we've received God's forgiveness yet refuse to pass it on, we're demonstrating that we don't truly understand what he has done for us in the first place. Until we do, we're going to keep struggling to do the same for others. No one could ever possibly owe us a debt greater than the one we owed God, yet God forgave us, and he continues to forgive us daily.

What do you do when you find yourself struggling to forgive?

You go back to all the times of your life when you've seen God give you mercy. You meditate on the cross. You look at how he's released so many people from bondage throughout history. You cultivate a life of remembering, reflecting on, and retelling the stories of how you and the people you know have been forgiven. And as you do, you'll be deepening your capacity to pass that forgiveness to others.

In 1989, Tim Keller planted Redeemer Presbyterian Church in Manhattan. Early in the life of the church, Keller noticed a visitor leaving quickly after each service. One day, he managed to intercept her before she was able to make her escape. It turned out she wasn't a Christian; she was only "exploring" Christianity.

Curious, Keller asked how she'd ended up at Redeemer.

So, she told him her story.

She worked for a large media company in Manhattan, and, shortly after starting, she'd made a mistake—the kind of mistake that gets you fired. But her boss took the blame for her error, which allowed her to stay in her role. It was unlike anything she'd ever experienced. She'd had bosses who'd taken credit for her successes but never one who'd taken the blame for her failure.

Puzzled, she later asked her boss, "Why did you do it?"

After some hemming and hawing, he explained, "I am a Christian. That means among other things that God accepts me because Jesus Christ took the blame for things that I have done wrong. He did that on the cross. That is why I have the desire and sometimes the ability to take the blame for others."[14]

That's what it looks like to be swept up in the forgiving flow.

What I love most about this story is his humility in admitting that the *desire* to take the blame and the *ability* to take the blame aren't always the same.

It's like that with forgiveness.

Even when we've grasped the mercy we've received from him and genuinely want it to flow to others, forgiveness still can feel out of reach. That's why we need to keep turning to our *source* and asking for help—like Corrie ten Boom did.

PRAYING "GIVE YOUR FORGIVENESS"

Corrie was a Dutch Christian who, along with her family, helped hide Jews from the Nazis during World War II. She survived Ravensbrück, the notorious concentration camp for women. After her release, she went on to share her story of faith, forgiveness, and resilience worldwide. One day, while speaking to an audience in Germany, her faith in the power of forgiveness was put to the test.

> It was at a church service in Munich that I saw him, the former S.S. man who stood guard at the shower room door in the processing center in Ravensbrück. He was the first of our actual jailers that I had seen since that time. And suddenly it was all there—the roomful of mocking men, the heaps of clothing, Betsie's pain-blanched face.
>
> He came up to me as the church was emptying, beaming and bowing. "How grateful I am for your message *Fräulein*," he said. "To think that, as you say, He has washed my sins away!"

> His hand was thrust out to shake mine. And I, who had preached so often to the people in Bloemendaal the need to forgive, kept my hand at my side.
>
> Even as the angry, vengeful thoughts boiled through me, I saw the sin of them. Jesus Christ had died for this man; was I going to ask for more? "Lord Jesus," I prayed, "forgive me and help me forgive him."
>
> I tried to smile, I struggled to raise my hand. I could not. I felt nothing, not the slightest spark of warmth or charity. And so again I breathed a silent prayer. "Jesus, I cannot forgive him. Give Your forgiveness."
>
> As I took his hand the most incredible thing happened. From my shoulder along my arm and through my hand, a current seemed to pass from me to him, while into my heart sprang a love for this stranger that almost overwhelmed me.
>
> And so I discovered that it is not on our forgiveness any more than on our goodness that the world's healing hinges, but on His. When He tells us to love our enemies, He gives, along with the command, the love itself.[15]

Corrie ten Boom allowed her connection to the Source to open up a channel in her life to flow to others. She wasn't depending on herself; she wasn't capable of that. But God was. This is why Jesus tells us to pray every single day, "Forgive us our debts, as we also have forgiven our debtors."

So, when the memory of a hurt you can't shake starts in on you again, take a page out of Corrie's book and connect with the *source.*

Pray, *Jesus, I'm not capable of forgiving. I've tried.*

Be my Source. Be for me what I cannot possibly be for myself.

You've shown me so much grace. Now carve me open as a channel so the grace you've given can flow to others.

Give your forgiveness through me.

Forgiveness is never easy. But it's how we resist becoming carriers of the very pain that wounded us in the first place. As Father Ronald

Rolheiser put it, "Any pain or tension that we do not transform we will retransmit."[16]

So instead of passing it on, we absorb it in cruciform love. We give back the very gift we've received: grace. Not because it's natural, but because we've been caught up in a larger story—one that breaks the cycle of violence and ends not in death but in life.

Resurrection isn't just the finale of Jesus' story. It's the pattern of ours. For those buried with Christ in death and raised with him to newness of life, dying and rising becomes a way of being. The old self gives way. The new creation takes root.

Forgiveness is how we join Jesus in saying, *The pain stops here.*

We confess. We release. We refuse to let bitterness harden into legacy.

We make space for something new to be born.

One prayer at a time. One day at a time. We don't just remember the resurrection, we practice it. And when we do, the goodness and power of heaven flows into our lives, giving us the capacity to pass it on to others.

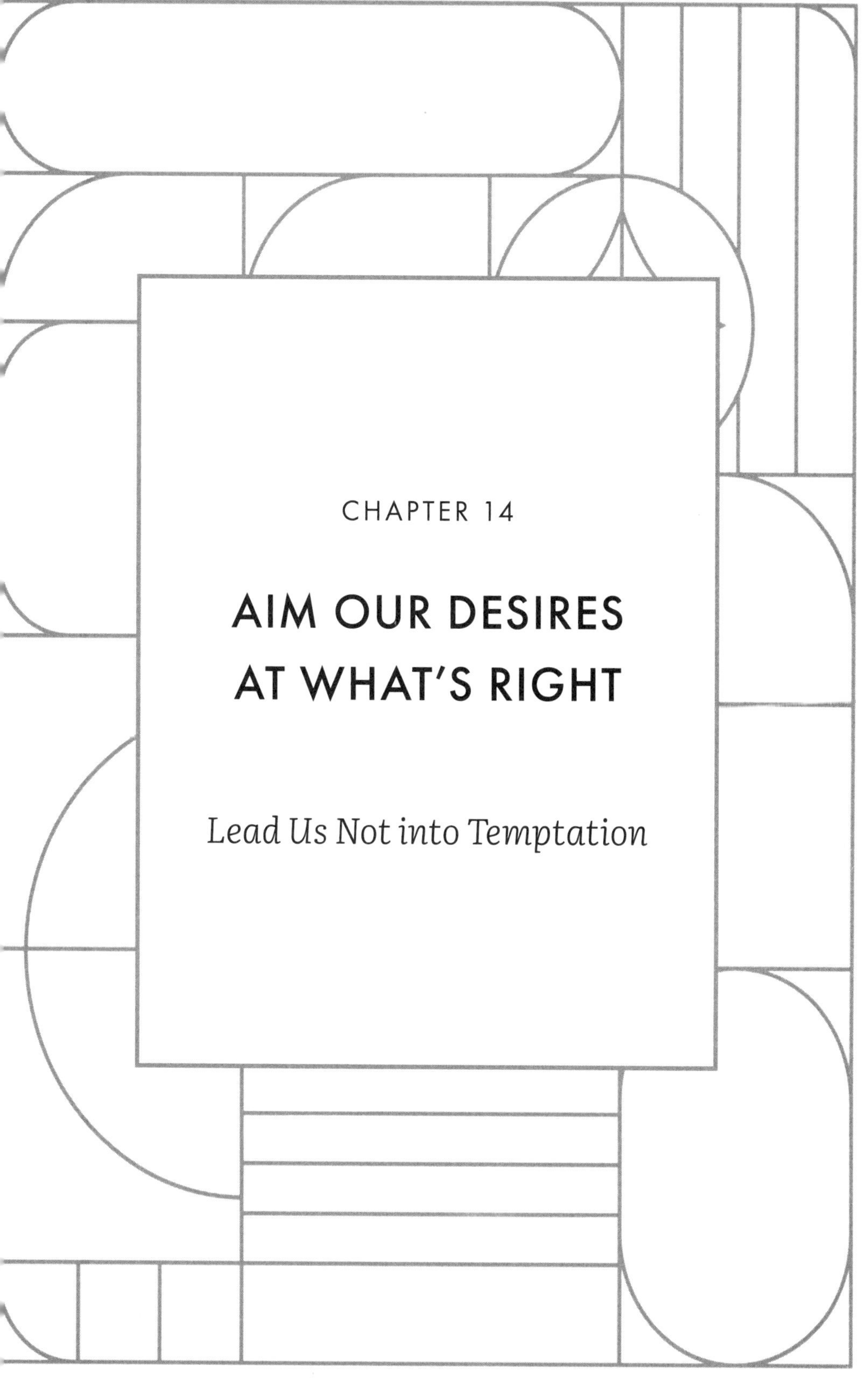

CHAPTER 14

AIM OUR DESIRES AT WHAT'S RIGHT

Lead Us Not into Temptation

BRAD NELSON

When I was five, my mom owned a cleaning business, which meant I spent a lot of afternoons entertaining myself in the empty homes of complete strangers. If I was lucky and the homeowners had kids, there were usually toys to play with. The only downside? Seeing all the cool stuff they had that I didn't.

Which brings us to the red bouncy ball.

You know the kind—it rockets into the air, smacks the ceiling, and ricochets around the room, knocking everything over.

I found it in a kid's bedroom, and it was exactly the kind of kinetic chaos my little heart longed to unleash. After deploying it indoors a few times, my mom promptly chased me outside where I spent hour after wondrous hour seeing how high I could bounce it.

That's when a thought hit me—*I want this ball to be mine.*

I knew it was wrong, but I really wanted that ball. *It's so small,* I told myself. *They'll never notice. And if they do, they'll just think it's lost.* So I pocketed it.

Turns out, that little ball was the center of "some kid's" universe. He *did* notice it was gone, and soon, I was back at the house—returning the ball, confessing my crime, and apologizing.

It was humiliating.

It was also my first real encounter with temptation.

Temptation is the whisper, that tug-of-war inside when we're drawn to do something we know is wrong. It's a universal experience, and it shows up in countless ways.

We're tempted to tell people off.

Spend money we don't have.

Give up when things get hard.

Cut corners when what's right is too costly.

Compromise sexually.

Keep our mouths shut instead of speaking up.

Or eat a gallon of ice cream instead of feeling our feelings.

Sometimes it's subtle. Other times it hits like a tsunami. But temptation always pits our self-control against the pull of the powerful desires that pulsate within. As theologian Philip Sheldrake wrote, "The human heart is a place of conflicting desire."[1]

Because Jesus was tempted in every way, just like us (Hebrews 4:15), he included this simple plea in the Lord's Prayer: "Lead us not into temptation but deliver us from evil."

It's an honest prayer—a confession that we're not as strong as we wish we were. We stumble. We wander.

But here's the good news: Jesus didn't just face temptation. He conquered it, again and again, standing firm where we often fail, and offering a map for our own battles. Jesus didn't leave us to muscle through temptation on our own; he pointed us to a deeper strength, the kind that comes from a reoriented heart.

In the kingdom of heaven, desire isn't the enemy. It's a powerful, God-given gift meant to be named, honored, and directed at what truly satisfies. As we pray Jesus' words and follow his way, we'll see our desires more clearly, unmask temptation for what it really is, and find the courage, clarity, and grace to keep moving forward.

DOES GOD CAUSE THIS?

The words "lead us not into temptation" are troubling. They seem to imply that there are times when God deliberately orchestrates circumstances that cause us to fail. But does God really do that?

After Jesus' baptism, the Gospel of Matthew says, "Jesus was *led by the Spirit* into the wilderness to be tempted by the devil" (4:1, emphasis added). I don't know about you, but that sure sounds like God leading Jesus into temptation!

Yet there's another well-known passage in the book of James that says, "When tempted, no one should say, 'God is tempting me.' For God cannot be tempted by evil, nor does he tempt anyone" (James 1:13).

Feeling confused yet? If so, you're not alone.

This is one of those places where understanding the original language is helpful because the Greek word for temptation, *peirasmos*, has layers of nuance.[2] It can also mean "trial or test." So, depending upon the context, this word can mean "temptation" or "testing" (either can be seen as "trials" because they're difficult). In some cases, *peirasmos* can mean both.

Tests are for our good and our growth. In the same way that you hold a hundred dollar bill up to the light to check its authenticity, testing helps reveal whether students have truly mastered the material and are ready to move to the next stage of learning.

But *peirasmos* can also mean "temptation" in the sense of enticing someone toward sin or wrongdoing. Unlike a test, temptation lures people off course. It prevents them from realizing their potential by tripping them up and keeping them stuck.

The critical distinction is that *God tests* and *Satan tempts.*

God has always tested those who partner with him to bring heaven here.

He tested Abraham (Genesis 22:1). *Will you trust me with your future?*

He tested the Israelites (Deuteronomy 8:2). *Will you trust me for tomorrow's bread?*

He tested Jesus. *Will you trust me to make you king even if it means a cross?*

And he tests us.

Testing can feel disorienting, like things aren't going the way they're supposed to. But ironically, tests are often a sign that we're moving in the right direction. This is why the apostle Peter told persecuted Christians, "Do not be surprised at the fiery ordeal that has come on you to test you, as though something strange were happening to you" (1 Peter 4:12).

Tests and trials come with the territory. If you dare to join Jesus in living out the Lord's Prayer, evil will come after you like it came after him. If you've said yes to Jesus, you've said yes to a life of testing.

Unfortunately, tests can be unpleasant—and that's when temptation whispers, *There's an easier way.* This is why we often feel attacked at pivotal moments.

For instance, Satan tempted Jesus at three key moments in his life:[3]

- in the wilderness after his baptism (Matthew 4);
- at Caesarea Philippi (Matthew 16); and
- in the garden of Gethsemane (Matthew 26).

In each case, Jesus was crossing a threshold into a deeper dimension of his calling.

So, if you're about to take a step of faith, don't be surprised if things suddenly get difficult or you're tempted in some way, because faithfulness generates opposition.

But not every temptation is a test.

The impulse to run a red light because you're late for a meeting probably isn't God's way of preparing you to bring heaven here. Besides, there are plenty of times when Satan doesn't have to resort to subtlety to pull us off course. The sad truth is, we wander there on our own.

In his famous sermon on faith, Frederick Buechner said,

> We are more than half in love with our own destruction . . . There is that in all of us which hungers for the license to be subhuman not just sexually but any other way that appeals to us—the license to use and exploit and devour each other like savages, to devour and destroy our own sweet selves. And if you and I are tempted to think we don't hunger for such things, we have only to remember some of the dreams we dream and some of the secrets we keep and the battle against darkness we all of us fight.[4]

Buechner was right: We really are more than half in love with our own destruction. But why? What is it in us that so often chooses what we know will undo us?

The answer lies in something more powerful than most of us realize: desire.

THE POWER OF DESIRE

Psychologists and theologians agree, there is an inner tug-of-war between our desires and our capacity for restraint. In his book *The Happiness Hypothesis*, psychologist Jonathan Haidt likens the brain to an elephant and its rider. The elephant is that animalistic, primal part of us that just wants what it wants: food, sex, and red bouncy balls that don't belong to us. Like an elephant, these desires are huge, possessing a seemingly limitless supply of raw power. If you could tap into that raw energy—like getting an elephant to move—you could profoundly shape a person's choices, habits, and direction in life.[5]

Nobody understands this better than advertisers. Car commercials show people living their *best life*—only because they're *in this sweet ride!* They're not just selling a car; they're selling how the car will make you feel. The best advertisements are aimed not at your head but at your heart, with messages that have been crafted to activate, harness, and direct your desires toward a particular end.[6]

Before my friend Shane became a pastor, he worked for Porsche Cars North America. After a while, it dawned on him that "the most effective, award-winning, and respected advertising is that which convinces consumers that a product or service will meet their spiritual and emotional needs. In essence, the best advertising is *a counterfeit gospel* (emphasis added)."[7]

That's what makes it so powerful and so dangerous. The same strategy that sells you cars can sell you lies.

This is how evil works: It hijacks our desires—convincing us to aim them at things that can't satisfy and will ultimately enslave us.

Faced with this inner conflict, many people choose what looks like a much safer path: They try to shut down desire altogether.

But our desires aren't going anywhere. They're always there humming just beneath the surface, waiting to be stirred. We can't outrun them, ignore them, or stuff them in a closet and hope they behave; suppressing them only amplifies their power, making them darker and more demanding.

So, if we can't eliminate desire, how do we keep it from taking over?

Thankfully, Jesus shows us the way.

TEMPTATION AND DISCERNMENT

Jesus' first encounter with temptation takes place after his baptism, and it's an echo of a much older story. He spent forty days in the wilderness—much like Israel spent forty years in the wilderness.

God led both into seasons of testing.

We discussed in chapter 10 how God provided daily manna, telling the Israelites to gather only enough for one day and to trust he'd provide again the next day. Later, Moses told them, "Remember how the LORD your God led you all the way in the wilderness these forty years, to humble and *test* you in order to know what was in your heart, whether or not you would keep his commands" (Deuteronomy 8:2, emphasis added).

Israel failed their test.

As Matthew described Jesus being led into the wilderness just like Israel was, he wanted it to be clear: Jesus was reliving Israel's story. He was going to get right what they got wrong.

The devil began with food: "If you are the Son of God, tell these stones to become bread" (Matthew 4:3).

On the surface, this was a reasonable temptation. Jesus was hungry. He was the Son of God. Later, he would miraculously multiply loaves to feed hungry people. Why shouldn't he do it now?

But Jesus saw through it: It wasn't really about bread. It was about fulfilling a need or a desire without following the direction and permission of his Father.[8]

He answered Satan with Scripture: "Man does not live on bread alone, but on every word that comes from the mouth of God" (Matthew 4:4; Deuteronomy 8:3).

Jesus 1, Satan 0.

Undeterred, Satan took Jesus to the highest point of the temple—most likely the southwest corner of the Temple Mount platform. When Herod the Great expanded the temple precinct, he designated the southwest corner the focal point of the city, making it the most prominent and dramatic location for Satan's temptation. If Jesus were going to win followers through spectacle, this would be the perfect place to do it.

There, Satan threw out a reckless dare: "If you are the Son of God," he said, "throw yourself down." Then he followed up with a quote from Psalm 91: "He will command his angels concerning you, and they will lift you up in their hands, so that you will not strike your foot against a stone" (v. 6).

Once again, Jesus discerned that the real temptation was about fulfilling a desire without following the direction and permission of the Father.

Jesus 2, Satan 0.

Sensing the clock ticking, Satan went for the jugular. He took Jesus to a high mountain and showed him all the kingdoms of the world. "All this I will give you," he said, "if you will bow down and worship me" (v. 9).

This final temptation is devastatingly strategic. Satan offered Jesus the very thing Jesus came to reclaim—all the kingdoms of the world—but *without the suffering of the cross.* No years of touching lepers or casting out demons. No confrontation with the religious leaders. No betrayal. And definitely no cross. It was the shortcut temptation—the promise of power without pain; a crown without a cross; glory without Golgotha.

But unlike Israel, Jesus stayed true, saying, "Away from me, Satan! For it is written: 'Worship the Lord your God, and serve him only'" (v. 10).

Final score: Jesus 3, Satan 0.

The first lesson Jesus showed us about resisting temptation is seeing the thing behind the thing. He didn't simply react to Satan's suggestions; he discerned what was really going on underneath. Satan was trying to entice Jesus to use his power and identity to pursue provision, prominence, and power on his own terms rather than the Father's. But Jesus knew Satan's offers weren't just about food or recognition. They were about trust, obedience, and the path to becoming who he truly was.

Evil doesn't invent new cravings; it distorts the good desires God has already placed within us. The ability to recognize how our desires are being hijacked is essential to resisting temptation.

Therapist Jay Stringer has done groundbreaking work on this, describing how unwanted sexual behavior often traces back to unmet desires in childhood—longings for connection, safety, and worth that were left unfulfilled or twisted in secret.

He explained, "After I hear my clients' present-day struggles, a second storyline often emerges rooted in the formative years of their childhood . . . The formative experiences of our childhood [loneliness, pain, sexual arousal, secrecy, and relational ambivalence] are all being repeated in our unwanted sexual behavior as adults."[9]

If you're wrestling with sexual temptation—or any temptation at all—there's always a thing behind the thing. This issue isn't just about the behavior; it's about the longing underneath. It is a deep, God-given desire to be seen, to be safe, to belong. Until we learn to name our desire and own it by aiming it in the right direction, we'll keep getting pulled off course chasing distorted versions of what we were made for.

As C. S. Lewis said, "Our Lord finds our desires not too strong, but too weak. We are halfhearted creatures, fooling about with drink and sex and ambition when infinite joy is offered us, like an ignorant child who wants to go on making mud pies in a slum because he cannot imagine what is meant by the offer of a holiday at the sea. We are far too easily pleased."[10]

Freedom begins not with willpower but with wisdom, the kind that can discern the thing behind the thing. So, whatever temptation has its claws in you, take a step back and simply ask, "If this isn't about sex, or money, or food, what's it really about? What's the deep longing underneath this broken impulse?"

If you can name it, you've got a much better chance of taming it.[11]

TEMPTATION AND BOUNDARIES

Not all temptation looks like obvious cravings. Sometimes it comes disguised as love, concern, or even loyalty, pulling us off course through the people closest to us. That's what happened when Jesus took his disciples to Caesarea Philippi, a town with a long history of pagan worship. It had a temple to the god Pan, a temple honoring Caesar as lord,[12] and a massive cave with a spring gushing up from underground—a cave some believed was a gateway to Hades, the underworld.

It's here that Peter first recognized who Jesus truly was: the Messiah, the Son of the living God (Matthew 16:16).

Jesus confirmed Peter's confession, then said, "You are Peter, and on this rock I will build my church, and the gates of Hades will not overcome it" (v. 18).

It's classic Jesus. He brought the disciples all the way to Caesarea Philippi so they could actually see the gates of Hades behind him when he delivered that line. It's like he was telling them, "I'm going to take my kingdom right into the heart of hell and defeat it, and I'm commissioning you to join me!" I'm sure the disciples had goose bumps.

But once Jesus started describing *how* he planned to do this, things got awkward. Hearing Jesus' intention to travel to Jerusalem to suffer and die, Peter pulled Jesus aside to rebuke him.

Generally speaking, rebuking Jesus is never a good idea.

Like everyone else, Peter expected the Messiah to be a military conqueror king. If anybody was going to suffer, it would be the Messiah's enemies! Peter didn't have categories for what Jesus was describing. Plus, Jesus was Peter's close friend and Lord; Peter didn't want to see him suffer. So Peter said, "Lord. . . . This shall never happen to you!" (Matthew 16:22).

Here Matthew meant for us to hear the faint echo of Satan's earlier temptation in the wilderness—*all the kingdoms of this world, pain-free.* It's like Satan was offering the same deal, except this time, it came from the lips of Jesus' close friend.

Once again, Jesus saw the situation for what it really was: Satan trying to lure him off God's path. So, Jesus resisted temptation by doing something simple yet profound. He drew a boundary.

"Get behind me, Satan!" he said (v. 23).

It may not sound like a boundary, but that's exactly what it was. Jesus recognized the old temptation, a crown without a cross, and drew a line. *This is not from God. I won't entertain it.*

Sometimes resisting temptation doesn't look like fighting; it looks like stepping away, removing yourself from what threatens to pull you off course.

Which brings us back to the elephant and the rider as Haidt described them.

The elephant represents our desires—powerful, emotional, and impulsive. Atop the elephant, the rider is the rational part of us responsible for things like planning, self-control, and delayed gratification. We usually count on the rider to help us make wise choices.

But when push comes to shove, the rider is no match for the elephant. Once the elephant decides to move, the rider can't stop it.

Willpower is an exhaustible resource[13]—we burn through it quickly. That's why the ice cream in your freezer doesn't tempt you at 7 a.m., but at 9 p.m., after a long, exhausting day of biting your tongue with customers, clients, and coworkers, your willpower is running on fumes. That's when temptation hits hardest.

The weary and depleted heart is easy prey for temptation—but this is often a blind spot for us.

In 2009, researchers at Northwestern University and the University of Amsterdam identified something they called *restraint bias:* the tendency to overestimate our ability to resist temptation.[14] The more confident we are in our willpower, the more likely we are to put ourselves in situations that drain our strength and increase our chances of giving in.

In other words, the more we trust our self-control, the more likely we are to lose it. That's why it's often wiser to reshape your environment than to try and rein in your desire.

If pornography is eating you alive, draw a boundary. Cut off unsupervised internet access. If you're wasting hours scrolling Instagram, take it off your phone. If money's burning a hole in your pocket, don't keep it there! This isn't about taming desire—it's about designing your life so desire doesn't run the show.

Jesus knew how temptation works—how easily we can be worn down or thrown off course. That's why he taught us to pray, "Lead us not into temptation."

Temptation is not just difficult—it's dangerous. Stay near it long enough, and it'll wear you down. As Jesus told his disciples, "Watch and pray so that you will not fall into temptation. The spirit is willing, but the flesh is weak" (Matthew 26:41).

If Jesus could say, "Get behind me," so can we.

And when it feels like temptation is more than you can handle, remember this promise: "No temptation has overtaken you except what is common to mankind. And God is faithful; he will not let you be tempted beyond what you can bear. But when you are tempted, he will also provide a way out so that you can endure it" (1 Corinthians 10:13).

Your willpower might be gone, but God isn't. He's with you in the struggle, and he always makes a way.

TEMPTATION AND WILLINGNESS

Luke's account of Jesus' wilderness temptation ends on an ominous note: "When the devil had finished all this tempting, he left him until an opportune time" (4:13). That moment would come in the garden of Gethsemane.

If you stand on the Temple Mount in Jerusalem and look east across the Kidron Valley, you'll see the Mount of Olives. Situated at the western base of the Mount of Olives is an old olive grove and the Church of All Nations. This area commemorates the traditional location of the garden of Gethsemane,[15] and it's the likely location where Jesus brought his disciples (minus Judas) after the Last Supper on the night before his crucifixion.

Instructing eight of his disciples to sit tight in one part of the garden, Jesus took his closest three disciples—Peter, James, and John—farther in and told them, "My soul is overwhelmed with sorrow to the point of death. Stay here and keep watch with me" (Matthew 26:38).

Going a little farther into the garden alone, Jesus began to pray, "My Father, if it is possible, may this cup be taken from me. Yet not as I will, but as you will" (v. 39).

What cup was Jesus referring to?

It's the cup of judgment described in Psalm 75:8: "In the hand of the Lord is a cup full of foaming wine mixed with spices; he pours it out, and all the wicked of the earth drink it down to its very dregs." This cup represented God's judgment that would be poured out on the wicked and disobedient. And it would be Jesus' "cup" to drink.

The anticipation of bearing all the pain, brokenness, heartache, chaos, and judgment was weighing him down. Luke even said, "Being in anguish, he prayed more earnestly, and his sweat was like drops of blood falling to the ground" (Luke 22:44).

We often picture Jesus with nerves of steel—cool, calm, and collected. We put so much emphasis on his divinity that we forget about his humanity. *He became like us.* He knows what it's like to dread tomorrow. He knows what it's like to count the cost or to want another way, an easier way.

And here's why the geography of Gethsemane matters. What most people don't realize is that the Judean desert—where Satan first tempted Jesus—is only a short stroll to the east. In this moment, Jesus could have risen to his feet, ascended the Mount of Olives, and slipped over the ridge—back into the very wilderness where Satan had offered him power without pain.

Was there a fleeting moment when he wondered, *Is the offer still on the table?* Did Jesus look around and think, *If I go east, I can accomplish my mission without any betrayal, torture, or death, but if I go west . . .* Could he even finish the sentence? Did the thought take the breath out of him?

Temptation is that fork in the road where we have to choose which path we're going to walk. Do we go east? Or do we go west? Do we take the easy way out and cut corners? Or do we stay faithful by walking the path God laid out for us?

Resisting temptation and walking our path God's way might mean waiting. It might mean taking the long way. It might even mean doing the one thing in the world you're most afraid to do.

Like telling the truth.
Having the conversation.
Taking a stand.
Sticking to your principles.
Showing up, even when you don't feel like it.

This is the way of Jesus. Ultimately, in the garden he prayed, "Father . . . not as I will, but as you will"—fully embodying the prayer he gave us to pray (Matthew 26:39).

Your kingdom come.

Your will be done.

What Jesus modeled in this moment is not willfulness but willingness.

Soon after, he was crucified, and John's gospel includes an important detail. "At the place where Jesus was crucified, *there was a garden*, and *in the garden* a new tomb, in which no one had ever been laid" (John 19:41, emphasis added).

Do you hear the echoed story?

Adam and Eve disobeyed God about a tree *in the garden*.

Jesus obeyed God about a tree (taking the form of a cross) *in the garden.*

Adam and Eve chose *willfulness* in the garden, and they failed the test.

Jesus chose *willingness.*

One reached for the tree.

The other submitted to it.

WALKING THE PATH HIS WAY

At one level, "lead us not into temptation" is about resistance. Push back at temptation, friends. Don't go down without a fight. Draw a boundary. Create space where obedience can grow.

But resistance is just the beginning. Faithfulness is not suppressing desire but surrendering it. It's not letting desire dictate the path but putting it in its rightful place at the foot of the cross.

Whatever temptation you're facing, look at it closely and name what's beneath it. Then surrender it to the one who authored your desires in the first place, even if that road leads to a cross.

If walking your path God's way means counting the cost, don't shrink back. It might mean quitting your job or leaving security behind to follow the call that won't leave you alone. It could be saying no to a deal that would compromise your soul or launching the thing God put in your heart, even when it costs you more than you expected.

Count the cost.

Stay the course.

Do not deviate from the path.

Walk it and walk it his way.

And know that when you do, you may just discover resurrection power meeting you at the edge of your obedience.

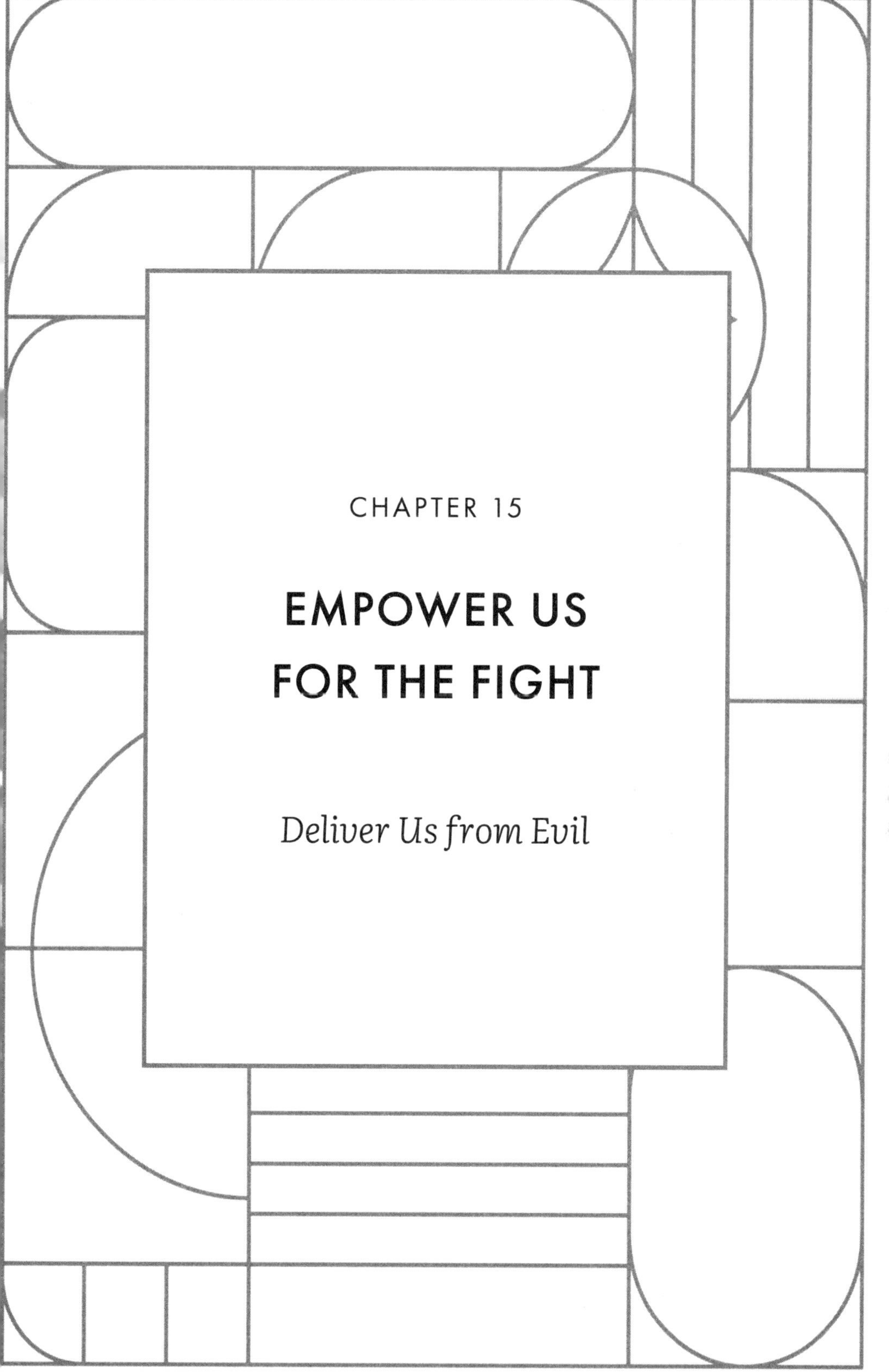

CHAPTER 15

EMPOWER US FOR THE FIGHT

Deliver Us from Evil

BRAD GRAY

The greatest shooter in basketball history is a four-time NBA champion with the Golden State Warriors: the legendary Steph Curry. He is also a devoted follower of Jesus. Before every game, Curry writes "Philippians 4:13"—his life verse—along with "I can do all things" on his basketball shoes with a Sharpie. It's a reminder he needs, because when you score like he does, you attract a lot of attention.

In a recent game against the Houston Rockets, Curry was relentlessly harassed and held to just three points. After the game, Curry's teammate Jimmy Butler reacted to the suffocating defense: "It's crazy to say, but he's used to it. He's been having this issue his whole career . . . I'm pretty sure this has been happening for sixteen straight years. It really angers me that he's on my team and he gets treated that way."[1]

That's the thing about being effective—when you're a threat, your opponents will go to great lengths to neutralize you.

Jesus offers a sobering reminder: If you pray everything else in his prayer and are becoming an effective member of God's kingdom, buckle up, because hell is going to oppose you with everything it has.

Opposition is part and parcel of the Christian life. Jesus experienced constant resistance.

Temptation.

Demonic opposition.

Religious and political pushback.

Even betrayal from those closest to him.

He wasn't kidding when he told his disciples, "'A servant is not greater than his master.' If they persecuted me, they will persecute you also" (John 15:20). Or as John also recorded Jesus saying, "In this world, you will have trouble. But take heart! I have overcome the world" (16:33).

The apostle Paul knew this firsthand (2 Corinthians 11:23–27). Have you ever stopped to think about all the opposition Paul faced?

He was imprisoned.
Beaten.
Stoned.
Mocked.
Shipwrecked.
Cold.
Naked.
Hungry.
Thirsty.

When describing his faith journey to the church in Corinth, Paul used one word over and over: "I have been in *danger* from rivers, in *danger* from bandits, in *danger* from my fellow Jews, in *danger* from Gentiles; in *danger* in the city, in *danger* in the country, in *danger* at sea; and in *danger* from false believers" (2 Corinthians 11:26, emphasis added).

Paul's brushes with danger weren't random; they were the inevitable results of warring with darkness. The same will be true for us.

Deliver us from evil is the daily acknowledgment that following Jesus isn't safe. Maybe you've heard the saying, "The safest place to be is in the center of God's will." Well, if that's the case, both Paul and Jesus set a terrible example. After all, it was God's will that led Jesus to the cross.

As Tim Mackie put it, "Jesus acknowledges that every day we need to be reminded that following Jesus is hard—that great tests and trials will come our way. But they are not signs that the Father has abandoned us. Paradoxically, they are signs that the Father is with us, and that he will deliver us—though for many, that deliverance may come through giving up their life. And that included Jesus."[2]

That's a tough message to accept in a culture addicted to safety. Most of us prefer certainty to faith. We want guarantees before we step out. We fall into the trap of making decisions based on fear instead of faithfulness. Yet Jesus doesn't want us to be naive to the fact that there's a war raging all around us.

Early in our marriage, my wife, Shallon, and I had a frustrating pattern. Nearly every Sunday morning before church, we'd get into a huge argument and end up skipping altogether, or we'd go in such a foul mood that we weren't able to focus. One day, we were discussing this with some friends when one of them asked, "Do you find it strange that this always happens *right before church*?"

The question hit like a lightning bolt. What if this was more than simple marital tension? What if we were experiencing something way more sinister—something that was trying to drive us away from one another and from God?

This happens, doesn't it?

Conflict flares up in a relationship at a critical moment.

Your mind is flooded by distractions and disruptions the minute you sit down to pray.

Right when you decide to take a step of faith, self-doubt threatens to derail you.

If you've ever felt like there are unseen forces working against you, it's because there are. Evil is real, and we're engaged in a spiritual war. "Deliver us from evil" is more than a plea for God's protection. It's a summons to wake up to the war, because the most difficult battles we face are the ones we don't even realize we're fighting.

Some of you are already cracking your knuckles, relishing the thought of confronting evil head-on. *Evil's going down,* you think. *We ride at dawn.*

Others of you are wondering if now's a good time to stop reading this book and gift it to your aunt who's into this sort of thing. Before you do, hear me out.

Evil and spiritual warfare often divide people into two camps. In the insightful words of C. S. Lewis, "One is to disbelieve in their existence.

The other is to believe, and to feel an excessive and unhealthy interest in them."[3]

As usual, Lewis was way ahead of his time. A 2009 Barna study revealed that 4 in 10 Christians don't believe the devil is real.[4] Most think he's a kind of symbol for evil rather than an actual, sinister presence. In our disenchanted, scientific world where anything that can't be observed, measured, or replicated is automatically suspect, the idea that our universe is pulsating with unseen realities—angels and demons duking it out in a cosmic spiritual battle—sounds childish.

But if we're going to turn a blind eye to things like the devil and spiritual warfare, we're going to have to turn a blind eye to Jesus and to verses like Ephesians 6:12: "Our struggle is not against flesh and blood, but against the rulers, against the authorities, against the powers of this dark world and against the spiritual forces of evil in the heavenly realms."

The other extreme is believing there's a demon behind every bush. This gives evil far too much credit, not to mention letting us off the hook for our own destructive choices.

The devil made me do it.

I'm not irresponsible; I'm afflicted by a spirit of procrastination.

There is a third category, and it's what most people fall into. Therapist Adam Young calls it the duck-billed platypus camp. (Didn't see that coming, did you?) He says, "Many of us believe in evil the same way we believe in the duck-billed platypus—we know it's out there, but although we acknowledge it in theory, we don't stop to ask how it affects us."[5]

Regardless of where each of us sits on the continuum, we all need Jesus' wisdom and insight about *how things actually are*. Praying "deliver us from evil" is one of the ways we can develop what N. T. Wright calls "a sober, realistic assessment both of the struggle we are engaged in and of the weapons at our disposal."[6]

The good news is, Jesus has already won the victory, and he hasn't left us defenseless. He's given us everything we need to stand firm in the fight.

THE DIVINE WARRIOR

When you picture Jesus, what comes to mind?

I'm guessing *warrior* wasn't your first thought—though the Bible does frame him as one. It's called the divine warrior motif. The Old Testament describes God fighting for his people against enemy nations, other gods, and the raging sea; the most common title it uses for God is Lord of Hosts, which means, "God of Armies." And the New Testament presents Jesus as the divine warrior who fights for his people, even though at first glance it doesn't seem that way.

He came as a man from Nazareth who walked the dusty trails of Galilee with a group of mostly teenage disciples in tow. He came eating and drinking, healing the sick, and welcoming sinners and tax collectors. It might not sound like much of a military strategy, but make no mistake—Jesus' mission was war.

Peter described Jesus' life by saying, "He went around doing good and healing all who were under the power of the devil" (Acts 10:38). John was even more blunt: "The reason the Son of God appeared was to destroy the devil's work" (1 John 3:8).

Three times in John's gospel, Jesus called Satan "the prince of this world," meaning Satan had seized illegitimate dominion over the earth (John 12:31; 14:30; 16:11). When Jesus announced, "The kingdom of heaven has come near" (Matthew 4:17), he was telling Satan, "Your time is up."

We discussed in chapter 8 how Satan tempted Jesus in the wilderness immediately after Jesus' baptism, because Satan viewed the baptism as an act of war. After that, Jesus went on the offensive. In Mark's gospel, Jesus' first act after gathering his disciples was casting a demon out of a man in the synagogue in Capernaum. When the demon encountered Jesus, it said, "What do you want with us, Jesus of Nazareth? Have you come to destroy us? I know who you are—the Holy One of God!" (Mark 1:24). In the ancient world, knowing the precise name of an individual suggested you were securing mastery over them.[7] So when the demon identified

Jesus as "the Holy One of God," it was actually taking a swing at Jesus, trying to exercise control over him.

Bad idea.

"Jesus rebuked him, saying, 'Be silent, and come out of him!'" (Mark 1:25 ESV).

English doesn't quite capture the power of Jesus' response. The Greek word translated as "rebuked"—*epitimaō*—suggests an "explosive blast."[8] And the Greek word translated as "be silent"—*phimoō*—can mean "to muzzle."[9] So Jesus blasted the demon with his word and slapped a muzzle on it. How awesome is that?

In Luke, Jesus healed a woman who'd been crippled by a spirit for eighteen years (Luke 13:11–16). When the religious leaders objected to him healing on the Sabbath, Jesus pushed back: "Should not this woman, a daughter of Abraham, *whom Satan has kept bound for eighteen long years*, be set free?" (Luke 13:16, emphasis added).

In another encounter, Jesus told the disciples, "Let us go over to *the other side* (Mark 4:35)," referring to the Gentile territory of the Decapolis. He might as well have said, "Let's go to the dark side." In the language of war, it was like crossing enemy lines into the realm of Satan.[10]

Once again, evil tried to stop Jesus in his tracks. While they were crossing the sea, a furious storm threatened to sink the boat. Guess what Jesus did?

He "rebuked the wind and said to the waves, 'Quiet! Be still!'" (Mark 4:39).

Mark recorded the exact same words here that we saw Jesus use to silence the demon in Capernaum: *epitimaō*, Jesus' explosive rebuke, and *phimoō*—(translated as "be silent" in Mark 1 and "be still" in Mark 4)—that's the forceful muzzling.

When Jesus and his disciples finally reached enemy territory, the first thing Jesus did was cast a legion of demons out of a man living among the tombs.

In another passage, Jesus spoke about his kingdom storming the gates of hell (Matthew 16:18).

In yet another, he implied that he'd come to bind up Satan and plunder his house (Mark 3:27).

Jesus' last and greatest battle took place at the cross, where Satan and Rome conspired together. As we've said, most people in Jesus' day expected the Messiah to come as a military conqueror—one who'd raise an army, crush the Romans, and reestablish an independent Jewish kingdom. When Jesus was crucified as an enemy of the state, most considered it proof that he was no Messiah.

Crucifixion was political theater, a terrifying form of propaganda designed to communicate Rome's ominous greatness. *We have the power of death. Stand in our way, and this will be your fate.* One ancient Roman writer boasted, "Whenever we crucify the guilty, the most crowded roads are chosen, where the most people can see and be moved by this fear. For penalties relate not so much to retribution as to their exemplary effect."[11]

The cross was Rome's most potent weapon.[12]

The tomb was death's last and greatest stronghold.

On Good Friday, Rome and evil conspired against Jesus by forming an axis of evil.[13]

You would expect this to be the end of the road. How does a man who walks in peace stand his ground against an Enemy who steals, kills, and destroys (John 10:10)?

At the cross and the empty tomb, Jesus absorbed the worst that evil could do and refused to respond in kind. Instead, he surprised it with creative grace, exposing it for the sham that it is. The resurrection was the "deeper magic," as C. S. Lewis described in *The Lion, the Witch, and the Wardrobe*: "When a willing victim who had committed no treachery was killed in a traitor's stead. . . . Death itself would start working backward."[14]

Jesus, the divine warrior, defeated evil not by killing but by being killed to show that death doesn't get the last word. Sacrificial, suffering love does.

Every exorcism was an invasion. Each time he rebuked the darkness, more of God's light came surging in. Every healing was territory reclaimed for God's kingdom!

To call him Master and fashion your life after his is to join in the fight. Friends, you need to know that baptism makes you dangerous to the dark forces of this world. When you enter the waters of baptism, you're not performing an empty ritual or simply getting a photo op with family and friends. It's a swearing in. You're entering the subversive service of the kingdom of God.

SATAN'S TACTICS

One of the first ways to wake up to the war is to know our Enemy. The Chinese military strategist Sun Tzu wrote, "If you know the enemy and you know yourself, you need not fear the result of a hundred battles."[15] Paul said something similar in his second letter to the Corinthians: "We are not unaware of his [the devil's] schemes" (2 Corinthians 2:11).

So what can we learn about our Enemy, his schemes, and how they're being deployed against us?

First and foremost, evil's ultimate goal is to ruin the glory of God, and human beings bear God's glory in a way nothing else in all of creation does—so we're its primary target.[16] We each reflect God's glory in a manner uniquely shaped by our individual gifts and abilities, so Satan and his demonic underlings study us, learning our strengths and vulnerabilities. Then they attack us in the places we're most dangerous to the forces of darkness, which are the same places we're most susceptible to darkness.

For instance, if your greatest contribution to bringing heaven here is your ability to truly see others and compassionately attune to them, don't be surprised when you find yourself feeling unseen. The longer you ruminate on that thought, the more resentment will build, until finally you think, *Why should I keep offering such goodness to people who won't offer it back?*

Our Enemy is cunning, distorting what's good, beautiful, and true in order to shut us down and sideline us in the fight.

Armed with this information, the devil implements his primary scheme—lies.[17] In fact, the Greek word for "devil," *diabolos*, is rooted in the idea of slandering or accusing.[18] Jesus didn't pull any punches when he described this fallen being: "He was a murderer from the beginning, not holding to the truth, for there is no truth in him. When he lies, he speaks his native language, for he is a liar and the father of lies" (John 8:44).

Lies are incredibly powerful. The most destructive ones contain just enough truth to be believable. At first, the Enemy's accusations seem convincing.

You're alone.
People can't be trusted.
This always happens.
You don't have what it takes.
You're not enough.
No matter how hard you try, it will never be good enough.

I'm guessing you could fill a sheet of paper with "the usual suspects" the devil uses to accuse you.

The problem is, if we don't learn to resist these lies, in time they'll mutate into default assumptions. They'll become the lens through which we see the world, and then we'll make the tragic jump from believing lies to living them.[19]

This is why the apostle Paul wrote, "The weapons we fight with are not the weapons of the world. On the contrary, they have divine power to demolish strongholds. We demolish arguments and every pretension that sets itself up against the knowledge of God, and we take captive every thought to make it obedient to Christ" (2 Corinthians 10:4–5).

In another letter, Paul encouraged believers to put on the full armor of

God so they could take their stand against the devil's schemes (Ephesians 6:11), and those are our marching orders today too.

There's so much depth and significance in every piece of armor Paul described, but I want to focus on the last one, because it's the weapon Jesus wielded against Satan more than any other: the Word of God.

THE WEAPON WE'VE BEEN GIVEN

When Jesus was tempted by Satan in the wilderness, he didn't rely on cleverness or charisma. He relied on God's Word. Each time Satan attacked, Jesus responded by quoting Scripture—and not just any scripture. He quoted from Deuteronomy, drawing directly from Israel's wilderness journey. Israel failed their test; Jesus passed his.

Yet Jesus was doing more than simply quoting Bible verses he'd memorized. He knew the story, the context, and the heart of God behind the words. At one point, Satan referenced Psalm 91:11 in a misleading way, saying, "He will command his angels concerning you . . ." Satan was ripping the passage out of context, using it to justify his own agenda.

But Jesus wasn't fooled. He knew that misusing Scripture is just as dangerous as disobeying it. It's not enough to know the Word—we have to know it in context, so we can recognize when it's being weaponized in a way God never intended.

Jesus didn't recite verses like magical incantations. He wielded them like a sword. And that sword has been placed in our hands.

Revelation 19 gives us a glimpse of the final battle—the ultimate clash between the forces of good and evil. And it's key to understanding how God calls us to fight.

In the text, the armies of heaven followed a rider on a white horse, and the rider's name is the Word of God. Additionally, "Coming out of his mouth is a sharp sword with which to strike down the nations" (v. 15). This is a deliberate clue about the kind of battle Jesus was waging, and it connects to multiple threads we've looked at before.

Let's lay them all out here:

Jesus was called "the Word made flesh" (John 1:14).

Jesus battled Satan in the wilderness by quoting Scripture.

Jesus muzzled demons and silenced storms, doing it with his authoritative word.

Jesus confronted the religious leaders by asking, "Have you not read?" followed by quoting Scripture.[20]

Even on the cross, in his final agony, he quoted Scripture.

When describing the armor of God, Paul instructed believers to take up the sword of the Spirit, which is the Word of God (Ephesians 6:17).

Hebrews 4:12 tells us, "The word of God is . . . sharper than any double-edged sword."

Revelation 19:15 describes the rider as the Word of God, wielding the sword of his mouth.

Again and again, God defeated evil—not with weapons, but with the powerful truth of his Word!

This has always been the battle plan. In the fourth century, a monk named Evagrius Ponticus categorized Satan's deceptions into eight types, which later formed the basis of the seven deadly sins. His solution? Scripture.

His book *Talking Back: A Monastic Handbook for Combating Demons*, is essentially an index of specific scriptures matched to specific lies. In the prologue, he offers this strategy: "In the time of struggle, when the demons war against us and hurl their arrows at us, let us answer them from the Holy Scriptures, lest the unclean thoughts persist in us, enslave the soul through sin, and plunge it into the death brought by sin."[21]

Now, it would be silly to think of God's Word as a kind of magical incantation—if you just say these words, evil goes away. That's not how this works. What Evagrius articulated, and what Jesus embodied, is that when you immerse your life in the wisdom of Scripture, *you become it.*

And this is exactly what Jesus did.

He read the text.
He studied the text.
He memorized the text.
He prayed the text.
He taught the text.
He lived the text.
He died the text.[22]

He was so immersed in God's Word that he became it, and the same can be true for us.

It's our turn to take up the fight. We have an Enemy. We don't have to look far to see the darkness at work in the world—the deception, division, and destruction at every turn. But the battle isn't simply out there. It's in us—the thoughts that whisper shame, the habits that keep us bound, the compromises that erode our faith. Evil works through lies, and its goal is our destruction.

But Jesus has given us his authority and shown us how to fight—not with rage, not with vengeance, not with the weapons of this world, but with truth. The same truth that silenced storms, muzzled demons, and broke the power of death. The Word of God is our weapon, and we must take it up and wield it. We must let it reshape us from the inside out.

So what do we do now?

Expose the lies. Name, with precision, the destructive thought patterns, fears, and false beliefs that keep replaying in your mind. What accusations does the Enemy hurl at you? Where has deception taken root? Call it out.

Arm yourself with Scripture. Search God's Word like your life depends on it—because it does. Find the exact truths that dismantle those lies. Write them down. Speak them aloud. Let them become the words that guide your mind and shape your soul.

Let truth transform you. Don't just read Scripture—breathe it. Meditate on it. Memorize it. Pray it. Let it sink deep into your bones, so when the Enemy comes, you don't just repeat words—you stand in them.

Like Jesus, you wield truth not as a distant idea, but as the very foundation of your being.

Let me finish by offering a simple but powerful practice.

First, identify a lie. What is a recurring narrative the Enemy uses to take you out? It could be anything.

It's always going to be like this.
I can't trust anyone.
This always happens to me.

We usually have four or five of these on repeat in our heads at any given moment. Start by identifying them.

Second, ask, "Where does it hurt?" What wound does that lie activate in your heart?

Rejection?

Significance?

Insecurity?

Third, search the Scriptures to find a specific passage that speaks directly to the lie. Then write it on an index card or a Post-it note and place it somewhere you'll see it every day. Make it the background on your phone. This is God's truth for you to hold on to.

Feeling invisible? Maybe you start praying Psalm 10:14: "You, God, see the trouble of the afflicted; you consider their grief and take it in hand."

Holding back at work because of your age? Maybe you start praying Job 32:6–8: "I am young in years, and you are old; that is why I was fearful, not daring to tell you what I know. I thought, 'Age should speak; advanced years should teach wisdom.' But it is the spirit in a person, the breath of the Almighty, that gives them understanding."

Whatever you need, you'll find it in the text.

Finally, speak it aloud. Soak in it. Immerse yourself in it, and allow it to rewire your inner world. Remember, Satan cannot stomach people who walk in truth, and the more God's truth takes root in you, the more the lies will begin to lose their grip on you. And you'll become someone who doesn't just read the Word but lives it.

Friends, this is how we join Jesus in his kingdom work. This is how we reclaim the ground the Enemy has taken and stand in the authority Christ has given us.

So step into the battle.

Name the lies.

Identify the wounds.

Take up the Word.

And let truth reshape you.

This is how we fight, not with swords or fists, but with truth.

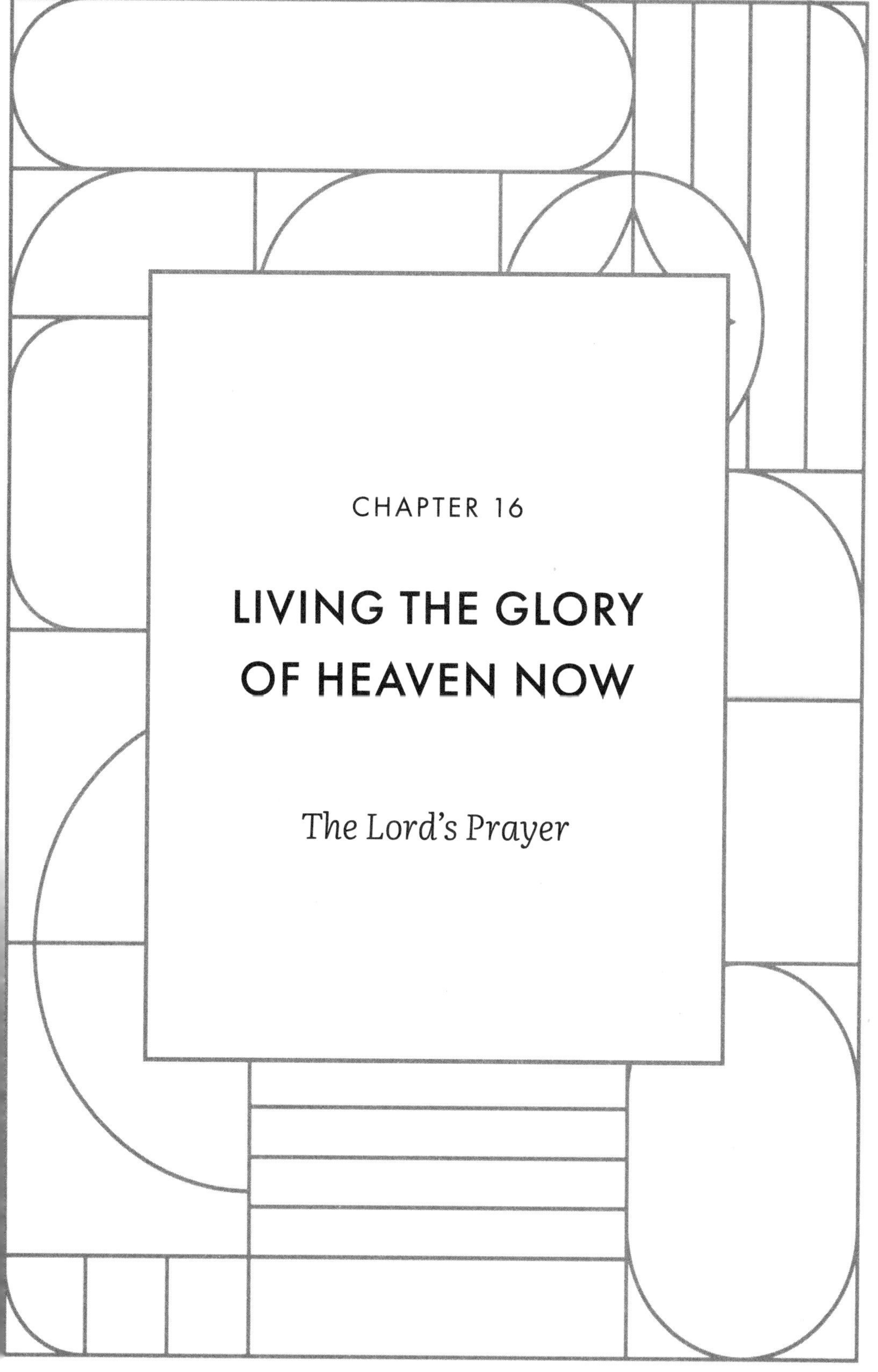

CHAPTER 16

LIVING THE GLORY OF HEAVEN NOW

The Lord's Prayer

BRAD GRAY AND BRAD NELSON

In the final months of his father's life, as dementia slowly unraveled his memory, the Scottish writer John Philip Newell noticed something remarkable. Though his father grew increasingly confused and forgetful, one thing remained: the instinct to bless.

The priestly blessing from Numbers 6:24–26—"The Lord bless you and keep you . . ."—had always been a favorite of his, and in those final days, it seemed to rise from the deepest part of him. Newell described it simply: His father wanted to give that blessing to everyone, everywhere, again and again. He had become the prayer he'd prayed for so long.

When it came time to sell the family car, which his father could no longer safely drive, Newell accompanied him to the dealership. At the close of the transaction, standing in the middle of the showroom, his father reached out, took the salesman's hand, looked him in the eye, and spoke the words that had lived in him for decades: "The Lord bless you and keep you; the Lord make his face shine upon you and be gracious to you; the Lord turn his face toward you and give you peace."

The young man's face crumpled into tears.

He would never forget that moment.

Neither would John Philip Newell. "If only I could be such a bearer of blessing in the world," he wrote.[1]

That's what happens when a prayer goes deep enough. It becomes what's left when all else fades away.

We began this journey by naming an ache: For many, the faith we're living isn't holding up. We're not as spiritually vibrant as we desire to be. Deep down, we're searching for something more. Something ancient and rooted. Something trustworthy. Something true.

That longing is what brought you here.

And now that we've walked through the prayer that can radically change your life, the question is simple: What will you do with it?

Will you let it shape the way you live and who you become?

In his book *A Hidden Wholeness*, Parker Palmer wrote, "There was a time when farmers on the Great Plains, at the first sign of a blizzard, would run a rope from the back door out to the barn. They all knew stories of people who had wandered off and been frozen to death, having lost sight of home in a whiteout while still in their own backyard."[2]

The Lord's Prayer is the rope Jesus ran for us—linking heaven and earth, giving us stability and direction in a disorienting world. It's the rope he held to with his life. And it's the one he invites us to hold to with ours. That's why we believe it's the single most important practice a follower of Jesus can commit to each day.

But holding the rope only matters if you actually walk the path.

In the opening chapter of this book, we named a danger: familiarity. Because the words of the Lord's Prayer are so well-worn, we can stop feeling their weight—but grasping the original context can shake us awake.

Here's the catch: You can know all that background and brilliance and still walk away unchanged.

This is why our goal throughout this book hasn't been to make you smarter, but to help you become more faithful. The only way that happens is for you to take what you've learned and apply it to your life.

Scripture constantly points toward walking out God's teachings. The Hebrew word *halakh* can be translated "to walk," "to go," or "to live"[3]—because in the biblical imagination, how you walk is how you live. It's where we get the expression, "walk the talk." Jesus finished the Sermon on the Mount by saying that very thing: "Everyone who hears these words of mine and *puts them into practice* is like a wise man who built his house on the rock" (Matthew 7:24, emphasis added).

It's when you apply what you've learned that you experience the transformational power of God in your life.

Jesus, of course, walked the talk. He embodied the prayer he taught, line by line, day after day. He wants us to do the same, which is why he told his disciples: "*When* you pray, say . . ." (Luke 11:2, emphasis added).

Not *if.*

Not *when you feel like it.*

When.

And we believe he meant it. So did the early followers of Jesus.

As we mentioned in the beginning of this book, the late first-century (or early second-century) discipleship training manual—the *Didache*—instructed Christians to pray the Lord's Prayer three times a day![4] It was the rhythm they lived by individually as well as communally.

HOW THE PRAYER ENDS

Some of you might be wondering, *Why isn't there a chapter in this book about "for yours is the kingdom and the power and the glory forever?" Isn't that how the prayer ends?*

Originally, no. The early church added those powerful closing words to make the prayer more conducive to liturgical use when they gathered as a community for worship. And it happened relatively early, as evidenced in the *Didache*, where the Lord's Prayer ends with "for yours is the power and the glory forever."[5] The inclusion of "the kingdom" came later, first showing up in biblical manuscripts in the fourth century.

The early church didn't choose these words at random. They likely drew them from another biblical prayer—one of David's—that shares similar themes with the Lord's Prayer: "Praise be to you, O Lord, the God of our father Israel, from everlasting to everlasting. Yours, O Lord, is the greatness and the power and the glory and the majesty and the splendor, for everything in heaven and earth is yours. Yours, O Lord, is the kingdom; you are exalted as head over all" (1 Chronicles 29:10–11).

It's a meaningful addition for several reasons, not the least of which is that the early believers saw Jesus' life and ministry as the fulfillment of David's prayer. Telling God, "for yours is the kingdom and the power and the glory forever" reminds us that we want to magnify his name and see his kingdom established.

It reminds us that he is the power at work in and around us; we depend on him as our source for all things, the one for whom nothing is impossible.

And it's his beauty, radiance, and glory that we long to see more of. We want to be part of filling the world with it—knowing, with deep joy, that a future shaped by his presence and peace is where the story is headed.

We resolve to start living the way we'll live forever with him *now.*

So here's our challenge to you: Commit your life to the work of bringing heaven here. This is what salvation was always meant to lead to—not escape, but embodiment. The prayer Jesus gave us isn't about "getting out of here." It's about bringing there, here.

Salvation isn't the finish line. It's the starting line. When you give your life to Jesus, you begin a journey of discipleship where you learn how to partner with Jesus in bringing heaven here. That's what this prayer does for you. It provides the blueprint and reminds you daily of what life is all about.

What would happen if this prayer sat at the center—fueling and animating every day for the rest of your life?

You'd live with laser-focused clarity on the things that matter.

You'd live with less anxiety and more trust.

You'd become a steward of your pain.

You'd begin to see from a higher perspective, sensing God's nearness in the details.

You'd start to radiate and reflect the holiness at the center of all things.

Your life would become a living advertisement for heaven.

You'd find meaning in the mundane, and the sacred in the ordinary.

You'd grow in gratitude and become more generous.

You'd be a breath of fresh, forgiving air in an angry, hostile world.

You'd awaken to the spiritual battle, and take your place in the fight.

When this prayer gets hold of you, it doesn't just inform you. It transforms you. And when you live it, line by line, it reshapes everything.

GETTING CREATIVE

There's no one right way to pray this prayer—just countless ways to let it form you. Here are a few practices that might help you make it your own.

One option is to pray the words slowly and thoughtfully, pausing to ponder the significance of each phrase and then praying accordingly.

Another possibility is to pray the prayer, but then focus on one phrase for each day of the week.

Sunday: Our Father.
Monday: In the heavens.
Tuesday: Holy be your name.
Wednesday: Your kingdom come, your will be done, on earth as it is in heaven.
Thursday: Give us this day our daily bread.
Friday: Forgive us our debts, as we also have forgiven our debtors.
Saturday: Lead us not into temptation but deliver us from evil.

You might choose to focus your prayers on a single line from the prayer for a full week.

Another option is to conclude your normal prayer time by saying the Lord's Prayer as a way of drawing everything to a close.

Or you could try the rhythm of the early church: Pray the entire prayer three times a day, like the *Didache* taught.

As we saw earlier in this book, prayer in the Hebrew mind was learned. The people recited the Psalms in order *to learn to feel* what the Psalms expressed. Once the prayers were in the people's hearts, they could begin freestyling like a jazz musician. They had access to those prayers and truths at any given moment and could apply them to any challenge.

So there's biblical precedent for choosing these particular words as your jumping-off point and then finding a way to make them your own.

AN EVOCATIVE EXAMPLE

The other day my wife and I (Nelson) were out on one of our evening walks when she turned to me and asked, "Here's what I want to know: How can the Lord's Prayer help me pray for our daughter?"

Our daughter is struggling. She's anxious—juggling AP and honors classes beneath the weight of academic pressure. She's a teenage girl navigating a world shaped by social media, where cruelty too often defines the terrain. Like so many her age, she feels misunderstood—adrift in the turbulence of adolescence.

As parents, it's gut-wrenching to watch someone we love hurt—and feel helpless to fix it. We try everything we know, and sometimes it still doesn't feel like enough.

My wife's question cut through the clutter: *So what?* When life gets messy, when the rubber meets the road, does this prayer change anything?

So I started riffing, like a jazz musician might—taking everything I'd learned and mapping the prayer onto the contours of our daughter's life. I didn't recite it; I walked it, line by line, placing her in God's hands all over again.

Our Father . . . the perfect parent. The one who sees her, knows her, loves her. God, parent her in the ways we can't. Love her with the kind of perfect love we're not capable of. And help us as her parents—tune our ears to hear her cries like you do. Be the God who hears the cries of your children and comes crashing in to rescue.

In the heavens . . . Lord, you see the big picture. When anxiety consumes her or heartbreak clouds her vision, help her rise above it. Help her zoom out. Let her see from your perspective—and let her feel your nearness. Remind us, too, that you're in control—that you see what we can't.

Holy be your name . . . Father, help us show her your beauty. May she be captivated by the healing, radiant goodness of a life centered on you. And may she represent you well in the world.

Your kingdom come, your will be done, on earth as it is in heaven . . . Jesus, let her glimpse heaven breaking through—today. Help her see how her life matters in your mission. Make her a walking, breathing doorway through which heaven touches earth.

Give her today her daily bread . . . Still her anxious thoughts. Remind her of your faithfulness in the past so she can trust you in the present. Let her heart shift from fear to gratitude—and from gratitude to generosity.

Forgive her debts, as she forgives her debtors . . . God, you see the cruelty—and you see how that same brokenness lives in all of us. Burn through it with your fierce, forgiving grace. May she be so overwhelmed by your mercy that she becomes a source of mercy for others—a breath of fresh, forgiving air in an angry, bitter world.

Lead her not into temptation, but deliver her from evil . . . Lord, have mercy. You know the Enemy is real and ruthless, that he strikes at the most tender places of her heart. Protect her. Shelter her. Deliver her. Be her refuge.

My words weren't polished. They were raw. Honest. Real.

You might know a thing or two about what that kind of prayer sounds like. It's what comes out of us when we pray for people we love.

Whenever you pray for your people next, don't overlook this prayer. Leverage it. Lean into it. It sustained Jesus. He believed it would sustain you too.

So picture this: a massive theater, completely dark. The stage is empty. Silent. Except for a single spotlight, cutting through the black, illuminating one simple stool at center stage. And on that stool sits a photograph.

If you're praying for yourself, it's a photo of you. If you're praying for someone else, it's that person. A child. A friend. A parent. Whoever it is, they're set up in the light—seen, held, centered.

As the light brightens, the image comes into focus: a life, fragile yet full of possibility. Broken, yes. But beautiful. Made to be an intersection of heaven and earth. And over that life, you begin to speak the words of the Lord's Prayer. Slowly. Intentionally. Line by line.

May these words bring you and the people you love closer to the love and care of the Father.

May they hold you when you can't stand.

May they steady your steps when the ground shakes.

May they guide your path with wisdom and wonder.

May they daily set your heart ablaze.

And may they empower you to bring heaven here.

ACKNOWLEDGMENTS

BRAD GRAY

So many people had a hand in bringing this project to life.

To Bryan Norman, our literary agent—thank you for shepherding both us and this project with the mind of a strategist, the heart of a pastor, and the care of a dear friend. You are a remarkable human being, and this book wouldn't exist without your steady belief and persistence.

To Carrie Marrs—thank you for believing in this project from day one and jumping in for the wild ride. You are an editorial savant and a consummate professional. Thank you for pushing us to write with greater clarity, depth, and impact. This book is infinitely better because of you.

To Rachel Buller and Jenn McNeil—thank you for bringing your brilliance to the editorial process. Your thoughtful feedback and meticulous attention to detail were invaluable.

To Damon Reiss, Caren Wolfe, Allison Carter, Lauren Ash, Elizabeth Hawkins, and the entire team at W Publishing Group and HarperCollins Christian—thank you for saying yes to this project and surrounding it with such extraordinary care. Your investment gave this book everything it needed to impact the lives of many.

To Randy Smith—a dear friend, mentor, and steady voice of wisdom in my life—thank you for the guidance and perspective you've offered throughout this journey. Your influence runs deep, and I'm profoundly grateful.

To April Gaddis—my remarkable executive assistant. Thank you for keeping everything together with excellence, grace, and heart. This book (and my sanity) are here in large part because of you.

To Marc Naugler, our creative director at Walking The Text—thank you for consistently bringing beauty and clarity to everything we create. And to Paul Weber, our director of strategic partnerships—thank you for your passion and tireless commitment to expanding the reach of our work. I'm grateful to run alongside you both.

To our Walking The Text board—Nate Young, Hala Saad, Rick Lyons, Jason Gianotti, and Gary Gray—thank you for your steady leadership, wisdom, and belief in our mission. Your support behind the scenes helped make this book—and so much more—possible.

To our Walking The Text community—thank you for your deep desire to understand the Word of God, your constant encouragement, and your faithful support that makes everything we do possible. You haven't just championed our work—you've helped shape and refine many of the ideas that found their way into this book.

To Joel Edwards, Daniel Kiedis, Lindsey Leatherman, Jen Lewis, Mark Ablaza, Aaron Seldon, and the rest of the talented team at Evolve Studios—thank you for pouring your creativity, care, and brilliance into *The Lord's Prayer* film and *The Sacred Thread* series. Your work didn't just bring those projects to life—it helped shape many of the ideas and language within these pages.

To my parents, my brother and his family, and my wife's family—thank you for your constant love, support, encouragement, and help along the way. Your steady presence and prayers have been a lifeline to me and my family.

To my wife, Shallon, and kids—Denyon, Aryah, Calyx, and Xyler—you are my greatest source of love, strength, and inspiration. Your patience, encouragement, and unwavering support carried me through this journey. I'm beyond blessed to walk through life with you, and I love you dearly.

To Brad Nelson—my coauthor, my best friend for over twenty-five years, and the other half of my brain—thank you. This book simply wouldn't exist without you. You carried the lion's share of the writing with grace, creativity, and brilliance. I'm profoundly grateful to have taken this journey with you.

And finally, to Jesus Christ—thank you for stepping into our world not only to die on our behalf, but also to live, and to show us what it truly means to embody the will and way of the Father here on earth. Thank you for giving us this prayer to daily guide our lives as we partner with you to bring heaven here. May you receive all the honor and glory—both now and forever!

BRAD NELSON

One of my favorite Hebrew words is *kaved*. It can mean "heavy" or "burdensome," but, in an ironic twist, it can also mean "glorious." When Moses' father-in-law visits him in Exodus 18 and sees the burden he's carrying, he tells him: You need to get some people to help you carry this load. I've always believed that shared burdens create glory. That feels like a fitting metaphor for this book. So many generous, talented, patient, and deep-hearted people have helped shoulder the load.

None more than my wife. To Trisha—my ideal reader and conversation partner. How many times did you come home from work, bags still in hand, only to listen as I read you the day's work aloud? Your love and support have been tireless. Your persistent challenge to keep asking, "So what?" has made this book far better than it would have been otherwise. You embodied the core insights of this book even as it was taking shape, modeling them in ways that inspired me daily. You have been generous and courageous in sharing your story. To you—whose gift is seeing others so deeply—may that same gift return to you tenfold. May you be truly seen for all your beauty and brilliance.

To my daughters—Braylen, Clara, and Charlotte. Thank you for being so generous with your stories and for filling our life together with so much laughter.

To my colleague and best friend, Brad Gray. People will never know what it cost you to see this project through. There are many things I admire about you—your brilliance, your perseverance, and the richness of your friendship. But they all pale in comparison to your faithfulness. Thank you for walking the talk and for inspiring and challenging the rest of us to do the same.

To Carrie Marrs, who has been a steady and dependable presence—someone I could lean on throughout this journey. Your empathy, advocacy, and emotional intelligence are rare gifts, and you bring them to bear masterfully. It's hard to be firm and friendly, patient and persistent all at once, but you manage to make it look effortless. Thank you for guiding this project with such a caring and skillful hand. Your instincts as a writer and your intuitive sense of what this book needed have truly made a world of difference.

To Damen Reiss, Caren Wolfe, Allison Carter, Lauren Ash, Elizabeth Hawkins, and the entire team at W Publishing Group and HarperCollins Christian. You brought the fun from the very first meeting. Thank you for all the encouragement, wisdom, and kindness you poured into this.

A special word of thanks to Rabbi Lawrence Kushner and Rabbi Albert Lewis, whose pastoral care and generosity during a sensitive season changed the trajectory of my life for the better.

Thanks also to my friends—Jeff Paulus, Balin Strickler, and Jordan and Vicki Ferrier—for reading early drafts and offering such thoughtful feedback. And to my brother-in-law Brett Newman, whose diligent meme-sending not only kept me sane but even inspired new content.

Finally, I want to thank the Spirit, who gives words and empowers those same words to become something living and true. It is a humbling privilege to be a conduit for that creative breath.

NOTES

Chapter 1: Strong Enough for the Weight of Life

1. U.S. Department of Health and Human Services, Office of the Surgeon General, *Our Epidemic of Loneliness and Isolation: The U.S. Surgeon General's Advisory on the Healing Effects of Social Connection and Community* (HHS, 2023).
2. William Butler Yeats, "The Second Coming," in *The Collected Poems of W. B. Yeats* (Wordsworth Poetry Library, 2008), 158.
3. The Gospels give us two versions—Matthew 6:9–13, a longer and more liturgical form; and Luke 11:2–4, a distilled version taught in response to the disciples' request. In this book, we'll be unpacking the fuller version found in Matthew.
4. William H. Willimon and Stanley Hauerwas, *Lord Teach Us: The Lord's Prayer and the Christian Life* (Abingdon Press, 1996), 18.
5. Didache 8.2–8.3, in Aaron Milavec, *The Didache: Text, Translation, Analysis, and Commentary* (Liturgical Press, 2003), 21.
6. Willard's words are often paraphrased. His exact quote is: "My hope is to gain a fresh hearing for Jesus, especially among those who believe they already understand him. In this case, quite frankly, presumed familiarity has led to unfamiliarity, unfamiliarity has led to contempt, and contempt has led to profound ignorance." Dallas Willard, *The Divine Conspiracy: Rediscovering Our Hidden Life In God* (HarperCollins, 1998), xiii.
7. Brad Gray, *The #1 Mistake Most Everyone Makes Reading the Bible*, 4th ed., e-book, 17. This e-book offers as case for context and provides a framework for engaging the six lenses of biblical context. Download for free at walkingthetext.com.
8. Eugene Peterson, *Eat This Book: A Conversation in the Art of Spiritual Reading* (Eerdmans, 2006), 71.

9. These are fifteen-to-twenty-minute video teachings on the Bible (also available as a podcast) found at walkingthetext.com. At the time of this book's release, we've created over two hundred of these.
10. We wrote the chapters together so the overall flow and ethos would be the same throughout. The only thing that changes is whose stories you're getting in each chapter.

Chapter 2: The One Who Cares for Us

1. Curt Thompson, *The Soul of Shame: Retelling the Stories We Believe About Ourselves* (InterVarsity Press, 2015), 138.
2. A. W. Tozer, *The Knowledge of the Holy* (HarperOne, 1978), 1.
3. For example, the first occurrence of the verb "love" (*ahav* in Hebrew) is in Genesis 22 in the account of the "binding of Isaac." It reads: "Then God said, 'Take your son, your only son, whom you love—Isaac—and go to the region of Moriah. Sacrifice him there as a burnt offering on a mountain I will show you'" (v. 2). This is one of the most intense stories in the Bible. It begins by God acknowledging Abraham's love for his son and then quickly moves to God instructing Abraham to sacrifice Isaac. Like I said, it's intense. Although we don't have the space here to provide a full, contextual analysis of this story, the connection is clear: Love, at its core, is sacrificial. As Jesus said in John 15:13, "Greater love has no one than this: to lay down one's life for one's friends."
4. Also referred to as the "Principle of First Occurrence," "The Law of First Use," or "Law of First Mention." These are modern titles we use to describe this ancient practice.
5. Straw is the key ingredient to keeping bricks intact when baked in the sun or heated. Thus, when Pharaoh ordered the Israelites to be given no more straw, and yet required them to meet their daily quota, they knew they were in serious trouble (see Exodus 5:17–21).
6. God didn't forget his covenant with Abraham, Isaac, and Jacob. The Hebrew word for "remember"—*zakhar*—also carries the idea of "advocating for." So to read that God "remembered" signified that God was about to act. See entry for זָכַר in Willem A. VanGemeren, ed., *New International Dictionary of Old Testament Theology and Exegesis (NIDOTTE)* (Zondervan, 1997), 1:1075–81.
7. Carmen Joy Imes, *Bearing God's Name: Why Sinai Still Matters* (IVP Academic, 2019), 27.

8. God said to Moses in Exodus 6:2–3, "I am the Lord [*Yahweh*]. I appeared to Abraham, to Isaac and to Jacob as God Almighty [*El Shaddai*], but by my name the Lord [*Yahweh*] I did not make myself fully known to them." Even though the name Lord (*Yahweh*) is used in the book of Genesis, it's here in Exodus 3 where God first reveals his proper name.
9. Rendered as "Lord" (in small caps) throughout the Old Testament, and first occurring here in Exodus 3:15, *Yahweh* (YHWH) is derived from the Hebrew verb *hayah*, which means "to be." For a helpful explanation on the confusing movement in this passage from "I am who I am" to "I am" to "Lord" (*Yahweh*), see John Mark Comer, *God Has a Name* (Thomas Nelson, 2024), 45–46.
10. Adele Berlin and Marc Zvi Brettler, eds., *The Jewish Study Bible: Second Edition* (Oxford University Press, 2014), 103–4.
11. Henri Nouwen, *The Return of the Prodigal Son: A Story of Homecoming* (Doubleday, 1992), 109.
12. On running the gauntlet of shame in his son's place, see Kenneth Bailey, *Poet and Peasant and Through Peasant Eyes: A Literary-Cultural Approach to the Parables in Luke* (Eerdmans, 1983), 182.

Chapter 3: The One We Can Count On

1. Andrew Peterson, "The Silence of God," *Love and Thunder* (Essential Records, 2003).
2. Laurence Hull Stookey, *Calendar: Christ's Time for the Church* (Abingdon Press, 1996), 79.
3. Paul H. Wright, *Rose Then and Now Bible Map Atlas* (Hendrickson, 2012), 28.
4. Rabbi Jonathan Sacks, *Covenant and Conversation, Numbers: The Wilderness Years* (Maggid Books, 2017), 394.
5. In this passage, the Hebrew word for "discipline" is *yasar*. While it does possess an element of "rebuke," the more pronounced meaning is of instruction. The comparison to a father's discipline indicates that the discipline, whether punitive or not, is administered with love as stated explicitly in Proverbs 3:11–12: "My son, do not despise the Lord's discipline and do not resent his rebuke, because the Lord disciplines those he loves, as a father the son he delights in."
6. Eugene Peterson, *The Pastor: A Memoir* (HarperOne, 2011), 207.
7. Krista Tippett and John O'Donohue, "John O'Donohue: The Inner

Landscape of Beauty," *On Being* (podcast), episode 1032, February 28, 2008, https://onbeing.org/programs/john-odonohue-the-inner-landscape-of-beauty/.

8. See entry for אִישׁוֹן in *NIDOTTE*, 1:386.
9. Frederick Buechner, "The Stewardship of Pain: A Meditation," Calvin Center for Excellence in Preaching, accessed May 13, 2025, https://cepreaching.org/audio-sermons/the-stewardship-of-pain-a-meditation-by-frederick-buechner/.
10. Leon Wieseltier, *Kaddish* (Vintage Books, 1998), epigraph.
11. Scot McKnight, *The Sermon on the Mount: Story of God Bible Commentary* (Zondervan, 2013), 173.

Chapter 4: The One Who Sits Above It All

1. Martin Rees, *Just Six Numbers: The Deep Forces That Shape the Universe* (Basic Books, 2000), 4.
2. Any Google search for "speed of light" will yield results for these numbers, such as this one: https://www.space.com/15830-light-speed.html.
3. Any Google search for this star will yield similar results, such as this one: https://www.technologyreview.com/2018/06/22/142160/this-is-how-many-people-wed-have-to-send-to-proxima-centauri-to-make-sure-someone-actually/.
4. No one knows for certain how many stars there are, which is why estimates are all over the place. Low estimates are around 100 billion. High estimates are around 400 billion as mentioned in this article: https://asd.gsfc.nasa.gov/blueshift/index.php/2015/07/22/how-many-stars-in-the-milky-way/.
5. The Virgo Galaxy is known as "Messier 87," and this NASA page indicates it's home to some several trillion stars: https://science.nasa.gov/mission/hubble/science/explore-the-night-sky/hubble-messier-catalog/messier-87/#:~:text=This%20enormous%20elliptical%20galaxy%20is,telescope%20most%20easily%20in%20May.
6. Ailsa Harvey and Elizabeth Howell, "How Many Galaxies Are There?", Space.com, February 1, 2022, https://www.space.com/25303-how-many-galaxies-are-in-the-universe.html.
7. Abraham Joshua Heschel, *I Asked For Wonder: A Spiritual Anthology* (Crossroads Publishing Company, 1983), 21.

8. Willard, *The Divine Conspiracy*, 71.
9. I'm borrowing this last line from Jonathan T. Pennington, who said this is an interview we did for Season 1 of *The Sacred Thread*. His book, *Heaven and Earth in the Gospel of Matthew* (Baker Academic, 2009) is one of the finest treatments about cosmology and the kingdom of heaven that's been done and helped shape several ideas used in this book.
10. Contemporary with Paul, we have other Jewish writings that talk about the heavens having five, seven, ten, or even more levels. For more on this, see Moyer Hubbard's comments on 2 Corinthians 12 in the *Zondervan Illustrated Bible Backgrounds Commentary: New Testament* (Vol. 3)—ed. Clinton E. Arnold (Zondervan, 2002), 254. Despite the differing views in Jewish literature, the three-fold division Paul references seemed common enough to him to warrant no further explanation.
11. Frank White, *The Overview Effect: Space Exploration and Human Evolution*, 4th ed. (Multiverse Media, 2023), 5.
12. For those of us who are bald, we've made God's job easier in this department!

Chapter 5: The One Who Is Always Near

1. David Brooks, *The Second Mountain: The Quest for a Moral Life* (Random House, 2019), xxvi.
2. Carl Sagan, *Pale Blue Dot: A Vision of the Human Future in Space* (Ballantine, 1994), 7.
3. Thomas Cahill, *Sailing the Wine-Dark Sea: Why the Greeks Matter* (Doubleday, 2003), 236.
4. Kyle Greenwood, *Scripture and Cosmology: Reading the Bible Between the Ancient World and Modern Science* (IVP Academic, 2015), 56.
5. Benjamin Foster, *Before the Muses: An Anthology of Akkadian Literature*, 3rd ed. (CDL Press, 2005), III.56, 763, quoted in Imes, *Bearing God's Name*, 34.
6. For a brilliant exploration of other ways the heavens and earth overlap, see Tim Mackie's presentation "Paradise Now," from the National Gathering of 24–7 Prayer USA, in Portland, Oregon, 2022, https://www.youtube.com/watch?v=HQlH-WfmZms.
7. Willard, *The Divine Conspiracy*, 256.
8. Lawrence Kushner, *God Was in This Place and I, I Did Not Know*, 25th anniversary ed. (Turner Publishing Company, 2016), 29.

9. More than a dozen sites have been proposed for the biblical Mount Sinai. Jebel Musa, in southern Sinai, is the traditional location and leading candidate. Its summit is 7,497 feet. Nearby is another candidate, Jebel Katherina, whose summit is 8,668 feet. See Gerald L. Mattingly, "The Location of Mount Sinai: A Southern Sinai View (Jebel Musa)," chap. 31 in Barry J. Beitzel, ed., *Lexham Geographic Commentary on the Pentateuch* (Lexham Press, 2022).
10. See entry for היה in Ludwig Koehler and Walter Baumgartner, eds., *The Hebrew and Aramaic Lexicon of the Old Testament (HALOT)* (Koninklijke Brill NV, 2000), 1:243–44.
11. Simone Weil, *Gravity and Grace*, trans. Emma Crawford (Routledge Classics, 2002), 117.
12. Wendell Berry, *The Gift of Good Land: Further Essays Cultural and Agriculture* (Counterpoint, 1981), 156.
13. To see Archbishop Desmond Tutu's speech at Davos, go to www.youtube.com/watch?v=sx89ZFRQ3xU.

Chapter 6: Center Us in Your Holiness

1. Raffi Berg, "Remains Found After Rare Shark Attack on Swimmer in Israel," BBC News, April 23, 2025, www.bbc.com/news/articles/c793rygrpjqo.
2. See entry for ἁγιάζω in Frederick William Danker, ed., *A Greek-English Lexicon of the New Testament and Other Early Christian Literature (BDAG)*, 3rd ed. (University of Chicago Press, 2000), 10.
3. See entry for קָדוֹשׁ in *HALOT*, 3:1066–67.
4. "An Emotional Visit to the American Cemetery of Colleville-sur-Mer," Normandy Tourism, accessed July 1, 2025, https://en.normandie-tourisme.fr/discover/d-day-and-the-battle-of-normandy/visit-american-cemetery/.
5. My own summary of content from BibleProject, "Holiness," *BibleProject*, video, 5:45, accessed May 13, 2025, https://bibleproject.com/videos/holiness/.
6. C. S. Lewis, *The Lion, the Witch, and the Wardrobe* (Harper Trophy, 1994), 80.
7. See entry for ירא in *HALOT*, 2:432–33.
8. Adam and Eve were afraid of God's approach after they had sinned (Genesis 3:8). Moses was afraid at the burning bush (Exodus 3:6). The

Israelites were afraid at Sinai and terrified of Moses' shining face (Exodus 20:18 and 34:30). Even dreams sent by God elicit fear.

9. "Holiness," *BibleProject*.
10. C. S. Lewis, *Mere Christianity* (Simon and Schuster, 1980), 183.
11. Jonathan Swift, Robert Demaria Jr., ed., *Gulliver's Travels*, (Penguin Books, 2003), 36.

Chapter 7: Make Us Your Representatives

1. This story, widely known as a modern parable and often attributed to Rabbi Akiva, does not appear in early rabbinic sources and has no verifiable origin in classical literature.
2. See entry for סְגֻלָּה in *HALOT*, 742. Additionally, Dr. Imes shared the concept of a *segullah* as "an authorized representative of the king" in our interview for Season 1 of *The Sacred Thread*.
3. Imes, *Bearing God's Name*, 33.
4. Paul H. Wright, *Holman Illustrated Guide to Biblical Geography: Reading the Land* (B&H, 2020), 84.
5. See entry for ירה in *HALOT*, 2:436–37.
6. Brooks, *The Second Mountain*, 58.
7. Baruch Sterman shared this with me during an interview we did for Season 1 of *The Sacred Thread*. The reason he gave the number for dying four blue threads is because each garment had four tassels—one per corner—so it took that many snails to dye one complete set. For a fascinating history on the rediscovery of "biblical blue," see Baruch's book *The Rarest Blue: The Remarkable Story of an Ancient Color Lost to History and Rediscovered* (Ptil Tekhelet, 2017).
8. Carmen Joy Imes, "Shattered: Top Ten Myths about the Ten Commandments," *Carmen Joy Imes* (blog), May 7, 2018, https://carmenjoyimes.blogspot.com/2018/05/shattered-top-ten-myths-about-ten.html.
9. See entry for נשׂא in *HALOT*, 2:724–27.
10. See entry for שׁוא in *HALOT*, 4:1424–26.
11. Jonathan Sacks, *To Heal a Fractured World: The Ethics of Responsibility* (Schocken Books, 2005), 68.
12. Leon Wieseltier, *Kaddish* (Vintage Books, 1998), epigraph.
13. J. H. Hertz, *The Pentateuch and Haftorahs* (Soncino, 1997), 519.

Chapter 8: Bring Your Good Rule Through Us

1. "Some 2.5 Billion TV Viewers Watch Princess Diana's Funeral," This Day in History, March 2, 2025, https://www.history.com/this-day-in-history/september-6/some-2-5-billion-tv-viewers-watch-princess-dianas-funeral.
2. "Netflix Reveals *The Crown* Viewing Figures for the First Time," BBC News, January 22, 2020, https://www.bbc.com/news/entertainment-arts-51198033.
3. Timothy Keller, "Jesus Our King," sermon preached at Redeemer Presbyterian Church, New York, NY, December 12, 1993, sermon audio available from Gospel in Life, YouTube, 41 min., 45 sec., https://www.youtube.com/watch?v=SjMGMUuNpZ4.
4. For a more detailed treatment of the structure of the Sermon on the Mount, see chapter 5 of Jonathan Pennington's fantastic book *The Sermon on the Mount and Human Flourishing: A Theological Commentary* (Baker Academic, 2017).
5. Ibid., 122.
6. See entry for צֶלֶם in *HALOT*, 3:1028–29.
7. Richard J. Plantinga, Thomas R. Thompson, and Matthew D. Lundberg, *An Introduction to Christian Theology* (Cambridge University Press, 2010), 184.
8. See entry for עָבַד in *NIDOTTE*, 3:303–08.
9. See entry for שׁמר in *HALOT*, 4:1581–84.
10. Numbers 3:7–8, 8:26, 18:7.
11. Eugene Peterson, *Under the Unpredictable Plant: An Exploration in Vocational Holiness* (Eerdmans, 1992), 12.
12. It's common to hear people say the kingdom is "already, but not yet." However, it's more biblically accurate to say the kingdom is "already, and even more to come!"
13. See entry for רחף in *HALOT*, 3:1219–20.
14. Chagigah 15a, *William Davidson Talmud*. You can access both the Hebrew and English at https://www.sefaria.org/Chagigah.15a.3?lang=bi https://www.sefaria.org/Chagigah.15a.3?lang=bi&with=all&lang2=en.
15. Willard, *The Divine Conspiracy*, 41.

Chapter 9: Reign in Our Little Spheres

1. Tobias S. Guggenheimer, *A Taliesin Legacy: The Architecture of Frank Lloyd Wright's Apprentices* (Van Nostrand Reinhold, 1995), vii.

2. Guggenheimer, *A Taliesin Legacy*, 9.
3. Ibid.
4. Willard, *The Divine Conspiracy*, 17.
5. Sacks, *To Heal a Fractured World*, 59.
6. Willard, *The Divine Conspiracy*, 56.
7. Andy Crouch, "The Three Callings of a Christian," blog, January 2015, https://andy-crouch.com/extras/the_three_callings.
8. Ibid.
9. Robert K. Chigangaidze and Patience Chinyenze, "What It Means to Say, 'A Person Is a Person Through Other Persons': Ubuntu Through Humanistic-Existential Lenses of Transactional Analysis," *Journal of Religion and Social Work: Social Thought*, 41, no. 3 (2022), 280–95, https://www.tandfonline.com/doi/abs/10.1080/15426432.2022.2039341.
10. "Vandals Cover Rio's Christ Statue with Graffiti," Reuters, April 16, 2010, https://www.reuters.com/article/world/vandals-cover-rios-christ-statue-with-graffiti-idUSTRE63F49G/#:~:text=The%20vandals%20covered%20the%20head,for%20what%20they've%20done.
11. I'm leaning on Praxis' concept of the redemptive frame. To read more, check out *The Redemptive Business: A Playbook for Leaders* by Praxis Labs (Praxis, 2021).
12. Dave Blanchard, Andy Crouch, and Scott Kauffman, *The Redemptive Business: A Playbook for Leaders* (Praxis Labs, 2021), 17.
13. I Like Giving is a nonprofit organization dedicated to inspiring lives of generosity. They turned Catherine's story into a beautiful short film called "I Like Car." with the help of Baas Creative. You can watch it here at I Like Giving's YouTube account, posted October 10, 2012, https://www.youtube.com/watch?v=LIASx_kTv8M.
14. This is from Glenn Packiam's Instagram post reflecting on Eugene Peterson's funeral, January 3, 2024, https://www.instagram.com/p/C1oDPgGrnFo/.

Chapter 10: Teach Us the Grace of Enough

1. N. T. Wright, *The Lord and His Prayer* (Eerdmans, 1996), 23.
2. Brooks, *The Second Mountain*, xii.
3. See entry for מָן in *HALOT*, 2:596.
4. I heard Walter Brueggemann make this quip once.

5. Walter Brueggemann, *Deep Memory, Exuberant Hope: Contested Truth in a Post-Christian World* (Fortress, 2000), 72.
6. Lois Tverberg, "Geshem—Drinking Rain from Heaven," En-Gedi Resource Center, July 2, 2015, https://engediresourcecenter.com/2015/07/02/geshem-rain-from-heaven/.
7. Lynne Twist, *The Soul of Money: Transforming Your Relationship with Money and Life* (Norton & Company Ltd., 2003), 43–44.
8. Philippians is part of what's called Paul's "Prison Letters." If Paul was writing Philippians from Rome (the majority view), he wasn't in "prison" per se. He was under what we call "light-chain house arrest" as he was awaiting trial under Nero, being guarded by a Roman soldier. If he was writing Philippians from Ephesus (the minority view), then he was likely in prison. Regardless of which one is correct, Paul was "in chains."
9. Jonathan Sacks, "To Thank Before We Think," *Covenant and Conversation: Yitro*, Rabbi Sacks Legacy, accessed June 18, 2025, https://rabbisacks.org/covenant-conversation/yitro/to-thank-before-we-think/.

Chapter 11: Be Our Ultimate Provider

1. Eugene Peterson, *Tell It Slant: A Conversation on the Language of Jesus in His Stories and Prayers* (Eerdmans, 2008), 183.
2. Juvenal, *Satire 10.77–81*. For the Latin and English, see *The Sixteen Satires*, 3rd ed., trans. Peter Green (Penguin Books, 2004), 78.
3. The problem for Rome was that Italy's conditions weren't conducive to growing grain. Growing grapes—sure. But grain? Not so much. With more than a million people in Rome, they had to import grain from around the Empire to meet its daily needs.
4. From Brad Gray's interview with Dr. Randall Smith for Season 1 of *The Sacred Thread.*
5. "The treasury of manna shall again descend from on high, and they will eat of it in those years" (2 Baruch 29:8), quoted in Gary M. Burge, *The NIV Application Commentary: John* (Zondervan, 2000), 197.
6. James K. A. Smith, *On the Road with Saint Augustine: A Real-World Spirituality for Restless Hearts* (Brazos, 2019), 82.
7. The Hebrew phrase here is *be'acharit* ("in behind") *hayamim* ("the days"). The key word in play is *acharit* ("behind"), which is connected to the Hebrew word *achor*, which means "back or backward." Hence, the literal translation of "in the behind days." Much thanks to my good friend,

Travis West, associate professor of Hebrew and Old Testament at Western Theological Seminary, for pointing this out to me several years ago. Travis also discusses this idea in his outstanding book, *The Sabbath Way* (Tyndale, 2025), 71.

8. Josef Hayim Yerushalmi, author of *Zakhor: Jewish History and Jewish Memory* (University of Washington Press, 1996), 5: "Altogether the verb *zakhar* appears in its various declensions in the Bible no less than one hundred and sixty-nine times, usually with either Israel or God as the subject, for memory is incumbent upon both."
9. John Gottman, *The Science of Trust: Emotional Attunement for Couples* (W.W. Norton, 2011), 176.
10. Ibid., 30.
11. Steve Jobs, "Steve Jobs' 2005 Stanford Commencement Address," Stanford, YouTube, posted March 7, 2008, accessed June 3, 2025, https://www.youtube.com/watch?v=UF8uR6Z6KLc.
12. Sometimes referred to as the Via Maris ("The Way of the Sea"), but many biblical geographers question the usage of Via Maris for this coastal highway. See Carl G. Rasmussen, *Zondervan Atlas of the Bible* (Zondervan, 2010), 32–33, as well as Anson F. Rainey and R. Steven Notley, *The Sacred Bridge: Carta's Atlas of the Biblical World*, 2nd ed. (Carta, 2014), 165–66.
13. Ronald Rolheiser, *The Holy Longing: The Search for a Christian Spirituality* (Image, 1999), 94.

Chapter 12: Make Us People of Release

1. Steve Carter, *Grieve, Breathe, Receive: Finding a Faith Strong Enough to Hold Us* (Thomas Nelson, 2024), 57.
2. Quoted in Stephen Post and Jill Neimark, *Why Good Things Happen to Good People: How to Live a Longer, Healthier, Happier Life by the Simple Act of Giving* (Broadway Books, 2007), 81.
3. Several of the key ideas in this chapter and the next are adapted from chapter 3 of Brad Gray's book *Make Your Mark: Getting Right What Samson Got Wrong* (FaithWords, 2014).
4. See entry for ἀφίημι in Moisés Silva, ed., *New International Dictionary of New Testament Theology & Exegesis* (Zondervan, 2014), 1:444–49.
5. As Paul wrote, "Do not repay anyone evil for evil. Be careful to do what is right in the eyes of everyone. If it is possible, as far as it depends on

you, live at peace with everyone. Do not take revenge, my dear friends, but leave room for God's wrath, for it is written: 'It is mine to avenge; I will repay,' says the Lord" (Romans 12:17–19). When Paul quoted God as saying, "It is mine to avenge; I will repay," he was referring to Deuteronomy 32:35. Additionally, perhaps Paul had Psalm 37:8 ("Refrain from anger and turn from wrath; do not fret—it leads only to evil") in mind when he was composing this section of Romans.

6. If you haven't read Bessel VanderKolk's *The Body Keeps the Score: Brain, Mind, and Body in the Healing of Trauma*, do yourself a favor and check it out.
7. This document, called the Septuagint, is especially helpful for understanding the connection between New Testament and Old Testament words. *Aphiēmi*, the word Matthew uses for forgiveness in Matthew 6:12, appears repeatedly in the passages about Jubilee.
8. "What Forgiveness Is and Isn't (The Lord's Prayer Pt. 4)," *BibleProject Podcast*, episode 3, June 3, 2024, https://bibleproject.com/podcast/what-forgiveness-and-isnt-lords-prayer-pt-4/.
9. N. T. Wright, *Jesus and the Victory of God* (Fortress, 1996), 271.
10. "Rabbi Dr. Abraham Twerski On Anger," JINSIDER, YouTube, February 25, 2009, 3 min., 53 sec., https://www.youtube.com/watch?v=hdj9MBZBLGU&t=131s.
11. Desmond and Mpho Tutu, *The Book of Forgiving: The Fourfold Path for Healing Ourselves and Our World* (HarperOne, 2014), 131.
12. Peterson, *Tell It Slant*, 186.

Chapter 13: Draw Us into the Forgiving Flow

1. Jeremy Clarkson, *Diddly Squat: A Year on the Farm* (Penguin Random House, 2021), 11.
2. Tim Keller, *The Reason for God: Belief in an Age of Skepticism* (Riverhead, 2008), 196.
3. This is a quote from the Babylonian Talmud (*b.* Yoma 86b, 87a), and it captures the rabbinic concern about unrepentant offenders who continue to repeat the same offenses. Although this statement comes after the time of Jesus, many scholars see it as reasonable evidence of what Peter likely believed and why he asked the question.
4. Furthermore, before the Bible had chapters and verses, *remez* functioned

like a "shorthand" that indicated where the teacher was drawing their illustration from. Much thanks to Dr. Randall Smith for this analogy.

5. This is the only place in the Hebrew Scriptures that contains both "seven" and "seventy-seven."
6. Brad Gray, *Make Your Mark: Getting Right What Samson Got Wrong* (FaithWords, 2014), 54.
7. Henri Nouwen, "Forgiveness: The Name of Love in a Wounded World," *Weavings: A Journal of the Christian Spiritual Life* 7, no. 2 (1992), 6–15.
8. Everett L. Worthington, Jr., "Six Ways to Deal With Someone Who Wronged You," *Greater Good,* May 15, 2023, https://greatergood.berkeley.edu/article/item/six_ways_to_deal_with_someone_who_wronged_you.
9. Despite this quote being referenced in numerous places, there is no known primary source—such as Jerome's letters or commentaries—that contains this exact wording in translation. Therefore, while the sentiment aligns with Jerome's deep connection to the Holy Land, the precise origin of the quote remains uncertain. However, it's really good (and accurate), so we're going with it!
10. As the crow flies, the distance between the Sea of Galilee and the Dead Sea is only sixty-five miles. But because the Jordan River "snakes" its way through the Jordan Valley to the Dead Sea, the actual distance it travels is 130 miles. See Paul H. Wright, *Holman Illustrated Guide to Biblical Geography: Reading the Land* (B&H, 2020), 118–21.
11. Sacks, *To Heal a Fractured World*, 41.
12. Parker Palmer, *The Promise of Paradox: A Celebration of Contradictions in the Christian Life* (Jossey-Bass, 1980), 33.
13. See entry אהב in *HALOT,* 1:18.
14. Tim Keller, *Every Good Endeavor: Connecting Your Work to God's Work* (Penguin, 2012), 219.
15. Corrie ten Boom, *The Hiding Place* (Chosen, 2006), 247–48.
16. Ronald Rolheiser, *Sacred Fire: A Vision for a Deeper Human and Christian Maturity* (Image, 2014), 251.

Chapter 14: Aim Our Desires at What's Right

1. Philip Sheldrake, *Befriending Our Desires*, 3rd ed. (Liturgical Press, 2016), xviii.
2. See entry πειρασμός in *BDAG*, 793.
3. If you're interested in a deeper exposition of these three moments of

temptation, check out BibleProject's podcast episode, "Does God Lead Us Into Temptation? (The Lord's Prayer Pt. 5)," BibleProject, episode 24, June 10, 2024, https://bibleproject.com/podcast/does-god-lead-us-temptation-lords-prayer-pt-5/.

4. Frederick Buechner, *Secrets in the Dark: A Life in Sermons* (HarperCollins, 2006), 67–69.
5. Jonathan Haidt, *The Happiness Hypothesis: Finding Modern Truth in Ancient Wisdom* (Basic Books, 2006), 4.
6. I learned this from reading James K. A. Smith. His book *You Are What You Love: The Spiritual Power of Habit* is a must-read (Brazos, 2016).
7. Shane Hipps, *The Hidden Power of Electronic Culture: How Media Shapes Faith, the Gospel, and Church* (Zondervan, 2005), 13–14.
8. Huge thanks to our friend Dr. Randall Smith for pointing out this subtle but significant distinction. If you'd like to hear more of Dr. Smith's incredible insights, check out his YouTube channel, One Hour. One Book.
9. Jay Stringer, *Unwanted: How Sexual Brokenness Reveals Our Way to Healing* (NavPress, 2018), xxi.
10. C. S. Lewis, *The Weight of Glory* (Harper, 2001), 26.
11. I'm borrowing the expression "name it to tame it" from the one and only Dr. Dan Siegel.
12. This temple was located either within the city or roughly two miles southwest of Caesarea Philippi at a site known today as Omrit.
13. Gary Keller with Jay Papasan, *The One Thing: The Surprisingly Simple Truth Behind Extraordinary Results* (Rellek, 2014), 63.
14. Loran F. Nordgren, Frenk van Harreveld, and Joop van der Pligt, "The Restraint Bias: How the Illusion of Self-Restraint Promotes Impulsive Behavior," *Psychological* 3, no. 2 (2009), https://heathbrothers.com/wp-content/uploads/2018/04/mktg_02_10_Nordgren.pdf.
15. Fun fact: It's never called the "garden of Gethsemane" in Scripture. Matthew and Mark call it "Gethsemane" (Matthew 26:36; Mark 14:32), Luke refers to the general location "Mount of Olives" (Luke 22:39), and John calls it a "garden" (John 18:1, 26).

Chapter 15: Empower Us for the Fight

1. Ishaan Bhattacharya, "Video Shows How Rockets Defended Stephen Curry and Held Him to Just 3 Points," Fadeaway World, April 7, 2025,

https://fadeawayworld.net/nba/golden-state-warriors/video-shows-rockets-defended-stephen-curry-held-him-to-3-points.

2. Tim Mackie Archives, "The Lord's Prayer [Matthew]–Tim Mackie (The Bible Project)," YouTube, 49 min., 55 sec., August 20, 2017, https://www.youtube.com/watch?v=LMmN8Ablo5s.
3. C. S. Lewis, *The Screwtape Letters* (Touchstone, 1996), 15.
4. "Most American Christians Do Not Believe That Satan or the Holy Spirit Exist," Barna Group, April 13, 2009, https://www.barna.com/research/most-american-christians-do-not-believe-that-satan-or-the-holy-spirit-exist/.
5. Adam Young, "Warfare Part 1: The Reality of a War Against Your Heart," *The Place We Find Ourselves* (podcast), July 1, 2019, season 3, episode 41, https://podcasts.apple.com/us/podcast/41-warfare-part-1-the-reality-of-a-war-against-your-heart/id1373926216?i=1000443371330.
6. N. T. Wright, *Paul for Everyone: The Prison Letters* (Westminster John Knox Press, 2002), 73.
7. William L. Lane, *The Gospel of Mark: The New International Commentary on the New Testament* (Eerdmans, 1975), 74.
8. See entry επιτιμάω in *BDAG*, 384. In his book *God Is A Warrior: Studies in Old Testament Biblical Theology Series* (Zondervan, 1995), Tremper Longman III points out that *epitimaō* is regularly used in the Septuagint to translate the Hebrew word *gāʿar* a word that can be translated as "an explosive blast."
9. See entry φιμόω in *BDAG*, 1060.
10. James Martin, "Crossing Enemy Lines," *TableTalk* magazine (Ligonier Ministries), May 1990, 34–35.
11. Quintilian, *The Lesser Declamations*, decl. 274, vol. 1, ed. and trans. D.R. Shackleton Bailey, Loeb Classical Library (Harvard University Press, 2006), 259.
12. For more on crucifixion and its use by the Romans, get Richard Horsley's book *Jesus and the Powers: Conflict, Covenant, and the Hope of the Poor* (Fortress, 2010).
13. Special thanks to Brian Zahnd for this turn of phrase!
14. C. S. Lewis, *The Lion, the Witch, and the Wardrobe* (Harper Trophy, 2000), 163.
15. Sun Tzu, *The Art of War*, trans. Thomas Cleary (Shambhala, 1988), 82.

16. Dan B. Allender, *Healing the Wounded Heart: The Heartache of Sexual Abuse and the Hope of Transformation* (Baker, 2016), 35.
17. John Mark Comer, *Live No Lies: Recognize and Resist the Three Enemies That Sabotage Your Peace* (Waterbrook, 2021), 18.
18. See entry διάβολος in *BDAG*, 226.
19. This quote is originally from David Benner, but I became aware of it through John Mark Comer's brilliant book *Live No Lies: Recognize and Resist the Three Enemies That Sabotage Your Peace* (Waterbrook, 2021).
20. See Matthew 12:3, 12:5, 19:4, 21:16, 21:42, and 22:31.
21. Evagrius of Pontus, *Talking Back: A Monastic Handbook for Combating Demons (Antirrhetikos)*, trans. David Brakke (Liturgical Press, 2009), 49.
22. Jesus' final words on the cross where direct quotes from Scripture. "My God, my God, why have you forsaken me?" (Matthew 27:45; Mark 15:34) is from Psalm 22:1. "Father, into your hands I commit my spirit" (Luke 23:46) is from Psalm 31:5. "It is finished" (John 19:30) is from Psalm 22:31. This last line of Psalm 22—usually translated in English as "He has done it"—can also be translated literally from the Hebrew as "It is finished."

Chapter 16: Living the Glory of Heaven Now

1. John Philip Newell, *The Rebirthing of God: Christianity's Struggle for New Beginnings* (Christian Journeys, 2015), 22.
2. Parker Palmer, *A Hidden Wholeness: The Journey Toward an Undivided Life* (Jossey-Bass, 2004), 1.
3. See entry הלך in *HALOT*, 1:246–48.
4. Didache 8.2–8.3, in Aaron Milavec, *The Didache: Text, Translation, Analysis, and Commentary* (Liturgical Press, 2003), 21.
5. Ibid.

ABOUT THE AUTHORS

BRAD GRAY is the president and CEO of Walking The Text, a nonprofit organization that creates digital media resources and study trips to Bible lands to help people understand the Bible in its original context. Brad is the co-creator and host of *The Lord's Prayer* film and *The Sacred Thread* series, as well as the author of *Make Your Mark: Getting Right What Samson Got Wrong*. He has lived and traveled extensively in the Middle East and has been leading study trips since 2010. Brad is also a national speaker, communication specialist, ordained minister, and former teaching pastor with over a decade of serving in the local church. He has a business management degree from Cornerstone University (Grand Rapids, Michigan), a master of divinity from Western Theological Seminary (Holland, Michigan), and a graduate certificate from Jerusalem University College in Israel. Brad and his wife, Shallon, live with their four children in the greater Nashville area.

BRAD NELSON is the content director at Walking The Text, where he curates *The Teaching Series*, a biweekly podcast and video series; leads trips to Bible lands; and is a writer for *The Sacred Thread*. He is a national speaker, writer, and communication specialist. Prior to joining Walking The Text, Brad spent seventeen years in pastoral ministry serving the local church in Grand Rapids, Michigan, and planting Brick City Church in Ocala, Florida. Brad has a history degree from Cornerstone University (Grand Rapids, Michigan), a master of divinity from Western Theological Seminary (Holland, Michigan), and has done additional graduate work at Jerusalem University College in Israel. He and his wife, Trisha, live with their three daughters in Greensboro, Georgia.

CONTINUE *your* JOURNEY

Alongside this book, we've created a feature film and an episodic series on the Lord's Prayer—designed to take you on a powerful, cinematic journey through the meaning and message of Jesus' words.

Visit **TheLordsPrayer.com**

Or scan the QR code to explore the full experience.